Solutions Manual to Accompany

SYNTHESIS AND OPTIMIZATION OF DIGITAL CIRCUITS

Giovanni De Micheli
Stanford University

McGraw-Hill, Inc.
New York St. Louis San Francisco Auckland Bogotá
Caracas LIsbon London Madrid Mexico City Milan Montreal
New Delhi San Juan Singapore Sydney Tokyo Toronto

Contents

Chapter 2

Background

2.1

Show that the adjacency matrix of a dag can be cast into lower triangular form by a row and column permutation.

Solution

Use the following procedure. Determine any enumeration of the vertices that is consistent with the partial order represented by the dag. Permute the rows and columns of the adjacency matrix according to the consistent enumeration.

The (permuted) adjacency matrix A is upper triangular, because any vertex, say v_i can only be adjacent to vertices that follow it in the consistent enumeration. Thus, $a_{i,j} = 0 \ \forall j \leq i$, and this holds for all i.

A lower triangular matrix can be obtained by transposing the upper triangular matrix, (which is equivalent to permuting the positions of the rows and columns), or directly by choosing a vertex enumeration that is the inverse of one consistent with the partial order represented by the dag.

2.2

Compute the longest path weights of the graph of Figure 2.11 (b) (in the textbook) by a modified Bellman-Ford algorithms where the min operator is replaced by a max operator. Show all steps.

Solution

Consider the graph of Figure 2.11 (b) in the textbook. The modified Bellman-Ford algorithm initializes the longest paths to: $s_0^1 = 0; s_1^1 = 3; s_2^1 = 1; s_3^1 = -\infty$.

At the first iteration (i.e. $j = 1$), the path weights are updated as follows:

$$
\begin{aligned}
s_0^2 &= \max\{s_0^1, s_3^1 + w_{3,0}\} = \max\{0, -\infty - 6\} = 0 \\
s_1^2 &= \max\{s_1^1, s_2^1 + w_{2,1}\} = \max\{3, 1 + 1\} = 3 \\
s_2^2 &= \max\{s_2^1, s_1^1 + w_{1,2}\} = \max\{1, 3 - 1\} = 2 \\
s_3^2 &= \max\{s_3^1, s_1^1 + w_{1,3}, s_2^1 + w_{2,3}\} = \max\{-\infty, 3 + 1, 1 + 4\} = 5
\end{aligned}
$$

At the second iteration:

$$
\begin{aligned}
s_0^3 &= \max\{s_0^2, s_3^2 + w_{3,0}\} = \max\{0, 5 - 6\} &= 0 \\
s_1^3 &= \max\{s_1^2, s_2^2 + w_{2,1}\} = \max\{3, 2 + 1\} &= 3 \\
s_2^3 &= \max\{s_2^2, s_1^2 + w_{1,2}\} = \max\{2, 3 - 1\} &= 2 \\
s_3^3 &= \max\{s_3^2, s_1^2 + w_{1,3}, s_2^2 + w_{2,3}\} = \min\{5, 3 + 1. 2 + 4\} &= 6
\end{aligned}
$$

At the third iteration:

$$
\begin{aligned}
s_0^4 &= \max\{s_0^3, s_3^3 + w_{3,0}\} = \max\{0, 6 - 6\} &= 0 \\
s_1^4 &= \max\{s_1^3, s_2^3 + w_{2,1}\} = \max\{3, 2 + 1\} &= 3 \\
s_2^4 &= \max\{s_2^3, s_1^3 + w_{1,2}\} = \max\{2, 3 - 1\} &= 2 \\
s_3^4 &= \max\{s_3^3, s_1^3 + w_{1,3}, s_2^3 + w_{2,3}\} = \max\{6, 3 + 1, 2 + 4\} &= 6
\end{aligned}
$$

Since the path weights match those computed at the previous iteration, the algorithm terminates successfully.

2.3

Prove that the $LEFT\_EDGE$ algorithm is exact.

Solution

Let $G(V, E)$ be an interval graph with chromatic number χ. Let the $LEFT\_EDGE$ algorithm color $G(V, E)$ with c colors. We want to show that $c = \chi(G)$.

We claim that the $LEFT\_EDGE$ algorithm assigns a color at each outer iteration to one element of all maximum cliques in the subgraph of $G(V, E)$ induced by the elements of the current list L. For the sake of contradiction, assume that there exists a maximum clique Q with no element being colored. Let S be the set of elements being colored at that iteration. Then, there exists an element $s \in S$ whose corresponding interval overlaps the intersection of intervals related to Q. Thus s belongs to the clique and we have a contradiction.

Therefore the clique number ω of the subgraph of $G(V, E)$ induced by the elements of the current list L decreases by one at each outer iteration. Consequently, the number of colors c equals $\omega(G)$. Since interval graphs are perfect, $\omega(G) = \chi(G)$ and thus $c = \chi(G)$.

2.4

Consider function: $f = ab + bc + ac$. Compute $\partial f/\partial b$, $\mathcal{C}_b f$, and $\mathcal{S}_b f$. Represent the function, the Boolean difference, the consensus and the smoothing on the three-dimensional Boolean cube.

Solution

Function $f = ab + bc + ac$ has $f_b = a + c$ and $f_{b'} = ac$, as shown in Figure 2.1 (a). The Boolean difference w.r.t. b is $\partial f/\partial b = f_b \oplus f_{b'} = (a + c) \oplus ac = a'c + ac'$. When $a'c + ac'$ is true, the value of f changes as b changes (Figure 2.1 (b)).

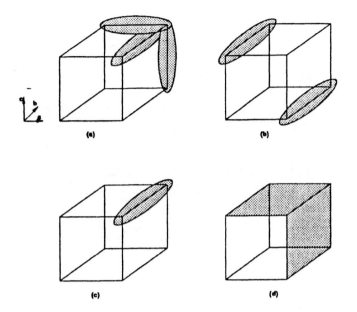

Figure 2.1: (a) The function $f = ab + bc + ac$. (b) The Boolean difference $\partial f/\partial b$. (c) The consensus $C_b(f)$. (d) The smoothing $S_b(f)$.

The consensus of f w.r.t b is $C_b(f) = f_b \cdot f_{b'} = (a + c)ac = ac$, and it represents the component of the function independent of b (Figure 2.1 (c)).

The smoothing of f w.r.t b is $S_b(f) = f_b + f_{b'} = (a + c) + ac = a + c$ and it represents the function when we drop the dependence of f on b (Figure 2.1 (d)).

2.5

Consider function: $f = ab+bc+ac$. Compute an expansion on the orthonormal basis $\{\phi_1 = a; \phi_2 = a'b; \phi_3 = a'b'\}$.

Solution

The generalized cofactors satisfy the following bounds:

$$ab + ac \ \subseteq \ o_1 \ \subseteq \ a' + b + c$$
$$a'bc \ \subseteq \ o_2 \ \subseteq \ a + b' + c$$
$$0 \ \subseteq \ o_3 \ \subseteq \ a + b$$

By choosing $f_{o_1} = ab + ac$, $f_{\phi_2} = a'bc$ and $f_{\phi_3} = a$ we can write:

$$
\begin{aligned}
f &= o_1 f_{o_1} + o_2 f_{o_2} + o_3 f_{\phi_3} \\
&= a(ab + ac) + a'b(a'bc) + a'(a) \\
&= ab + ac + a'bc \\
&= ab + bc + ac
\end{aligned}
$$

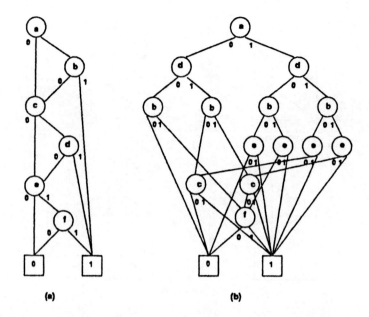

Figure 2.2: (a) ROBDD for variable order (a, b, c, d, e, f). (b) ROBDD for variable order (a, d, b, e, c, f).

2.6

Consider the function: $f = ab + cd + ef$. Determine the variable orders that minimize and maximize the size of the corresponding OBDDs.

Solution

An ordering of the variables that minimizes the number of vertices is: (a, b, c, d, e, f). Only 6 internal vertices are needed. An ordering of the variables maximizes the number of vertices is: (a, d, b, e, c, f), requiring 14 vertices. The corresponding ROBDDs are shown in Figures 2.2 (a) and (b) respectively.

2.7

Consider functions: $f = ab + bc$ and $g = ac$. Draw the corresponding OBDDs and determine the ROBDD corresponding to $f \oplus g$. Use variable order (a, b, c).

Solution

The ROBDDs of $f = ab + bc$ and $g = ac$ are shown in Figures 2.3 (a) and (b) respectively, for the ordering of variables (a, b, c). Recall that $f \oplus g = ite(f, g', g)$, as shown in Table 2.2 of the textbook.

Consider the construction of the ROBDD of the function $f \oplus g$ with variable order (a, b, c). Let a be the top variable. Then $ite((ab+bc), (a'+c'), (ac)) = ite(a, ite(b, c', c), ite(bc, 1, 0))$. This means that the ROBDD with top variable a has a right child corresponding to $ite(b, c', c) = b \oplus c$ and a left child corresponding to $ite(bc, 1, 0) = bc$. By using b as top variable for the left child, we can represent it as $ite(b, ite(c, 1, 0), ite(0, 1, 0)) = ite(b, c, 0)$, or equivalently by the ROBDD of Figure 2.3 (c). Similarly, by using b as top variable for the right child, we

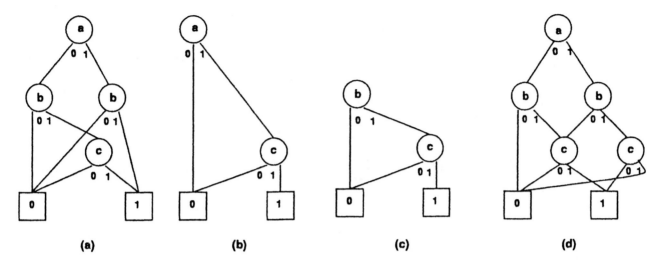

Figure 2.3: (a) ROBDD of $f = ab + bc$. (b) ROBDD of $g = ac$. (c) ROBDD of bc. (d) ROBDD of $f \oplus g = abc' + ab'c + a'bc$.

can represent it as $ite(b, ite(1, c', c), ite(1, c, c')) = ite(b, c', c)$, whose corresponding left child is represented by c and right child by c'. Note that since a vertex corresponding to variable c is already present within the ROBDD representing bc, which is now the left child of the root, this vertex is used also as left child of the ROBDD for $ite(b, c', c)$. The overall ROBDD for $f \oplus g = abc' + ab'c + a'bc$ is shown in Figure 2.3 (d).

2.8

Design an algorithm for detecting if $ite(f, g, h)$ is a constant. Explain why such algorithm is preferable to the regular ITE algorithm.

Solution

The following algorithm is a modification of the ITE algorithm that returns one of the following values $\{0, 1, n\}$, where n indicates that the ROBDD does not represent a constant. The rationale is that the ROBDD rooted at any internal vertex is a constant if and only if both its children represent equal constants. The following algorithm returns the value n as soon as a condition for the ROBDD not representing a constant is detected. Thus the algorithm is preferable to the regular ITE algorithm, because its computational cost is less in average.

```
ITE_CONSTANT(f, g, h){
        if (terminal case)
                return (r = trivial result);              /* 0 or 1 or n ; n means non-constant */
        else {
                if (computed table has entry {(f, g, h), r})   /* exploit previous information */
                        return (r from computed table);
                else {
                        x = top variable of f, g, h;
                        t = ITE_CONSTANT(f_x, g_x, h_x);
                        if ( t == n )
                                return (n);
                        e = ITE_CONSTANT(f_x', g_x', h_x');
                        if ( e == n )
                                return (n);
                        if ( t ≠ e)
                                return (n);
                        Update computed table with {(f, g, h), t};
                        return (t);
                }
        }
}
```

Chapter 3

Hardware modeling

3.1

Design a model of one-bit full-adder in structural VHDL, incorporating the half-adder model of Example 3.2.1. Include the interface description.

Solution

You need two half-adders and an OR gate. The structural description of the half-adders is reported in Example 3.2.1 of the textbook.

```
entity FULL_ADDER is
        port(a, b, c: in bit; sum, carry: out bit);
end FULL_ADDER;

architecture STRUCTURE of FULL_ADDER is
        component HALF_ADDER
                port (x, y: in bit; hsum, hcarry: out bit);
        end component;
        component OR2
                port (x, y: in bit; o: out bit);
        end component;
        signal ca, p, q: bit;
        begin
                G1: HALF_ADDER
                        port map (a, b, ca, p);
                G2: HALF_ADDER
                        port map (c, ca, sum, q);
                G3: OR2
                        port map (p, q, carry);
end STRUCTURE;
```

3.2

Design a model of a four-bit adder in behavioral and in data-flow VHDL. Include the interface description.

Solution

The description of the four-bit adder in behavioral VHDL.

```
package NEWINT is
   subtype int4 is integer range 0 to 15;
end NEWINT;

use work.NEWINT.all;
entity ADDER4 is
  port(a, b : in int4; ci : in bit;
       o : out int4; co : out bit);
end ADDER4;

architecture BEHAVIOR of ADDER4 is
begin
  process (a, b, ci)
    variable result: integer;
  begin
    if (ci = '0') then
      result := a + b;
    else
      result := a + b + 1;
    end if;
    if (result > 15) then
      co <= '1';
      o <= result - 16;
    else
      co <= '0';
      o <= result;
    end if;
  end process;
end BEHAVIOR;
```

The description of the four-bit adder in data-flow VHDL.

```
entity ADDER4 is
  port(a0, a1, a2, a3, b0, b1, b2, b3, c0 : in bit;
       o0, o1, o2, o3, co : out bit);
end ADDER4;
```

```
architecture DATAFLOWBEHAVIOR of ADDER4 is
   signal  ci1, ci2, ci3 : bit;
begin
   o0 <= (a0 xor b0) xor c0;
   ci1 <= (a0 and b0) or (c0 and b0) or (c0 and a0);
   o1 <= (a1 xor b1) xor ci1;
   ci2 <= (a1 and b1) or (ci1 and b1) or (ci1 and a1);
   o2 <= (a2 xor b2) xor ci2;
   ci3 <= (a2 and b2) or (ci2 and b2) or (ci2 and a2);
   o3 <= (a3 xor b3) xor ci3;
   co <= (a3 and b3) or (ci3 and b3) or (ci3 and a3);
end DATAFLOWBEHAVIOR;
```

In addition, we report here a structural version, using the following library gates: XOR2 (xor gate with two inputs), AND2 (and gate with two inputs), OR2 . (Extension to the problem)

For each one bit adder we need two XOR2 gates, two AND2 gates, and one OR2 gate.

```
use work.all;
entity ADDER4 is
   port(a0, a1, a2, a3, b0, b1, b2, b3, c0 : in bit;
        o0, o1, o2, o3, co : out bit);
end ADDER4;

architecture STRUCT of ADDER4 is
   component ADDER
     port (a, b, cin : in bit; o, cout : out bit);
   end component;
   signal ci1, ci2, ci3 : bit;
begin
   U1 : ADDER port map (a0, b0, c0, o0, ci1);
   U2 : ADDER port map (a1, b1, ci1, o1, ci2);
   U3 : ADDER port map (a2, b2, ci2, o2, ci3);
   U4 : ADDER port map (a3, b3, ci3, o3, co);
end STRUCT;

entity ADDER is
   port(a, b, ci : in bit;
        o, co : out bit);
end ADDER;

architecture STRUCT1 of ADDER is
   component AND2
     port (a, b : in bit; c : out bit);
   end component;
```

```
  component OR2
    port (a, b : in bit; c : out bit);
  end component;
  component XOR2
    port (a, b : in-bit; c : out bit);
  end component;
  signal ca, ps, pc : bit;
begin
  G1 : XOR2   port map (a, b, ps);
  G2 : AND2   port map (a, b, ca);
  G3 : AND2   port map (ci, ps, pc);
  G4 : XOR2   port map (ci, ps, o);
  G5 : OR2    port map (ca, pc, co);
end STRUCT1;
```

3.3

Design a model of the recursive filter of Example 3.2.4 in behavioral VHDL.

Solution

Differently from Silage, we have to insert a clock in the VHDL model to represent the delay. The following is the description of the recursive filter of Example 3.2.4 in behavioral VHDL.

```
entity IIR is
  port(x, a1, a2, b1, b2 : in integer;
       clock : in bit;
       y : out integer);
end IIR;

architecture BEHAVIOR of IIR is
begin
  process
    variable mid, mid1, mid2: integer := 0;
  begin
    wait until clock'event and clock = '1';
    mid2 := mid1;
    mid1 := mid;
    y <= mid + a2 * mid1 + b2 * mid2;
    mid := x + a1 * mid1 + b2 * mid2;
  end process;
end BEHAVIOR;
```

3.4

Consider a circuit that returns the integer addition of three 8-bit numbers, i.e. whose behavior is $x = a + b + c$. You have available only 1-bit full-adder cells. Neglecting the carry in and carry out signals, design a structural model of the circuit using 15 full-adders, and model it in your favorite HDL using metavariables. Show a block diagram and draw a bipartite graph representing the module/net structure.

Solution

a[0..7], b[0..7], c[0..7]

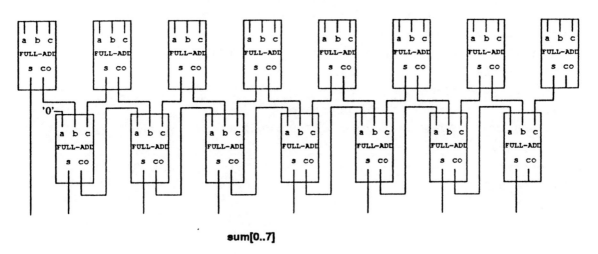

sum[0..7]

Figure 3.1: Structure of the 3-bit adder.

The structure of the circuit is shown in Figure 3.1.

The structural description of the one-bit full adders is assumed to be the same as in the solution to Problem 3.1.

```
package BIT_ARRAY is
   type BIT8 is array(0 to 7) of bit;
end BIT_ARRAY;

use work.BIT_ARRAY.all;

entity ADDER3 is
   port(a, b, c: in BIT8; sum: out BIT8);
end ADDER3;

architecture STRUCTURE of ADDER3 is
   component FULL_ADDER
      port(a, b, c: in bit; sum, carry: out bit);
   end component;
   signal co, co2 : BIT8;
```

```
    signal s : BIT8;
    signal s0 : bit;

begin
    -- first generate the top 8 full adders
    s0 <= '0';
    G1 : for I in 0 to 14 generate
      G2 : if (I < 8) generate
        FULLADD : FULL_ADDER port map(a(I), b(I), c(I), s(I), co(I));
      end generate;
      -- next hook up the 9th full adder, which is unique
      G3: if I = 8 generate
        FULLADD : FULL_ADDER port map(s0, co(0), s(1), sum(1), co2(0));
      end generate;
      -- finally generate the last six
      G4: if (I > 8) and (I < 15) generate
      FULLADD : FULL_ADDER port map(co2(I-9),co(I-8),s(I-7),sum(I-7),co2(I-8));
      end generate;
    end generate;
    sum(0) <= s(0);
end STRUCTURE;
```

The bipartite graph representing the module/net structure of the circuit is shown in Figure 3.2. The edges are labeled with composite names based on the inputs to the adders in the bottom row of Figure 3.1. (Of course, other labeling schemes could be used, but the net structure would remain the same.)

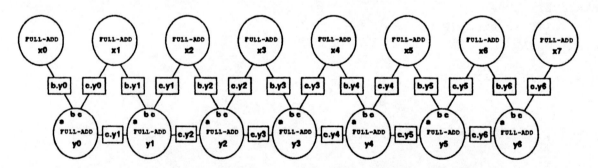

Figure 3.2: Bipartite graph showing module/net structure of the circuit.

The structure of the circuit including the carry in and carry out signal is shown in Figure 3.3. The corresponding VHDL code is similar to the above, with AND , OR and EXOR gates added appropriately.

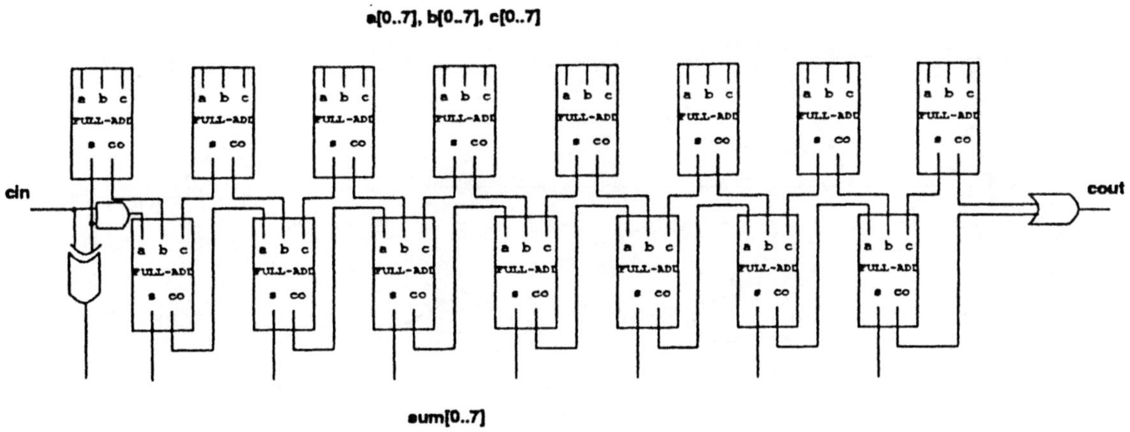

a[0..7], b[0..7], c[0..7]

Figure 3.3: Structure of the 3-bit adder considering carry in and carry out.

3.5

Consider the following model fragment:

$$x = ac + de$$
$$y = a + b$$
$$w = p + a$$
$$z = q + b$$
$$p = ac + ad + e$$
$$q = ap + b$$

Draw the corresponding logic network graph, while considering a, b, c, d, e as primary input variables and x, y, w, z as primary output variables.

Solution

The logic network graph representing the model fragment given is shown in Figure 3.4.

3.6

Consider a circuit that solves numerically (by means of the *backward Euler method*) the following differential equation: $y'' + 3xy' + 3 = 0$ in the interval $[0, a]$ with step-size dx and initial values $x(0) = x$; $y(0) = y$; $y'(0) = u$. Design a behavioral model in the VHDL language. Then draw the data-flow graph of the inner loop. Eventually, sketch the sequencing graph for the entire model.

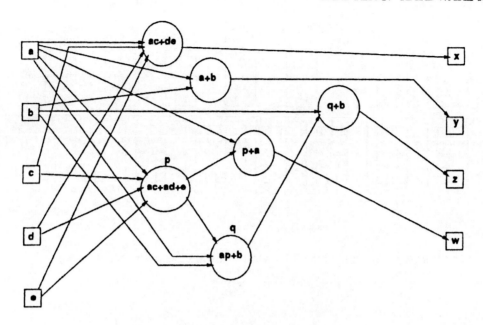

Figure 3.4: Logic network graph for problem 3.5.

Solution

Let $u = y'$. Then: $u' = -3xu - 3$. The backward Euler method uses the following approximation: $x_{n+1} = x_n + x'_{n+1}dx$. Thus, the backward Euler iteration is defined as follows: $u_{n+1} = u_n + (-3x_{n+1}u_{n+1} - 3)dx \implies (1 + 3x_{n+1}dx)u_{n+1} = u_n - 3dx \implies u_{n+1} = \frac{u_n - 3dx}{1 + 3x_{n+1}dx}$

$x_{n+1} = x_n + dx.$

$y_{n+1} = y_n + u_{n+1}dx.$

The following VHDL program successively calculates values for y.

```
package MYPACK is
  subtype INT8 is integer range 0 to 255;
end MYPACK;


use work.MYPACK.all;


entity DIFFEQ2 is
  port (dx_port, a_port, u_port : in INT8;
        y_port : inout INT8;
        clock, start : in bit);
end DIFFEQ2;


architecture BEHAVIORAL of DIFFEQ2 is
begin
  process
    variable x, a, y, u, dx, x_new, y_new, u_new : INT8;
```

```
  begin
    wait until start'event and start = '1';
    x := 0; y := y_port; a := a_port; u := u_port; dx := dx_port;
    while (x < a) loop
      wait until clock'event and clock = '1';
      x_new := x + dx;
      u_new := (u - 3*dx)/(1 + 3*x_new*dx);
      y_new := y + u_new*dx;
      x := x_new; u := u_new; y := y_new;
    end loop;
    y_port <= y;
  end process;
end BEHAVIORAL;
```

The data-flow graph of the inner loop is shown in Figure 3.5, and the sequencing graph in Figure 3.6. The root sequencing graph entity is shown in Figure 3.15 of the textbook.

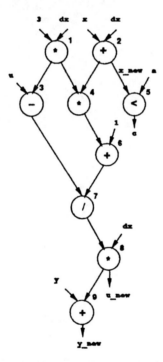

Figure 3.5: Data-flow graph for the loop body.

3.7

Design a model of a circuit (in your favorite HDL) that reads two numbers, computes their greatest common divisor by Euclid's algorithm, and returns this value. The circuit should operate every time a signal start is raised. Draw then the corresponding sequencing graph.

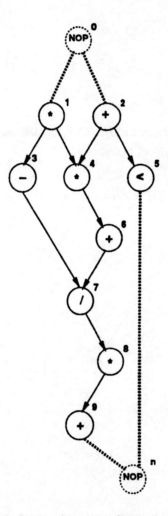

Figure 3.6: Sequencing graph for the loop body.

Solution

The gcd model described in this example consists of two input ports, one output port, and a one-bit input port that enables the gcd model when the value is low.

The gcd model can be enabled by setting start='1'. The output gcd_output will be evaluated as gcd(x, y) based on the input values of x and y. If start='0', then the output will be evaluated to be zero.

```
entity GCD is
 port (x, y              : in integer;
        start            : in bit;
        gcd_output       : out integer);
end GCD;

architecture GCD of GCD is
begin
  process(x, y, start)
    variable xvar,yvar :  integer;
  begin
    xvar := x;
    yvar := y;
    if ((xvar = 0) or (yvar = 0)) then
      gcd_output <= 0;
    end if;
    -- The GCD factorization takes place only if start = 1
    if (start = '1') and (xvar /= 0) and (yvar /= 0) then
      while (xvar /= yvar) loop
        -- Loop till the numbers are equal
        if (xvar < yvar) then
          yvar := yvar - xvar;
        else
          xvar := xvar - yvar;
        end if;
      end loop;
      gcd_output <= xvar;
    else
      gcd_output <= 0;
    end if;
  end process;
end GCD;
```

The sequencing graph corresponding to the gcd VHDL model is shown in Figure 3.7.

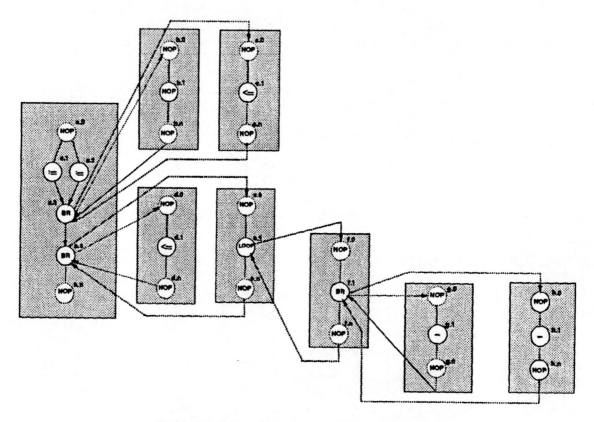

Figure 3.7: Sequencing graph for VHDL gcd model.

3.8

Consider the data-flow graph of Figure 3.11. Apply the following optimization techniques: (i) operator-strength reduction; (ii) common subexpression elimination. Draw the optimized data-flow graph.

Solution

Using the node numbers of Figure 3.11 to assign temporary variables with the same numbers to the operations' outputs, we begin with a data-flow graph corresponding to the following code:

```
t1 = 3 * x
t2 = u * dx
t6 = 3 * y
t8 = u * dx
x1 = x * dx
t3 = t1 * t2
t7 = t6 * dx
y1 = y + t8
c = x1 < a
t4 = u - t3
u1 = t4 - t7
```

After applying the optimization technique of operator-strength reduction, we get the following code:

```
t5 = x << 1
t1 = t5 + x
t2 = u * dx
t9 = y << 1
t6 = t9 + y
t8 = u * dx
x1 = x * dx
t3 = t1 * t2
t7 = t6 * dx
y1 = y + t8
c = x1 < a
t4 = u - t3
u1 = t4 - t7
```

After applying the optimization technique of common subexpression elimination, we get the following code:

```
t12 = x << 1
t1  = t12 + x
t2  = u * dx
t13 = y << 1
t6  = t13 + y
x1  = x * dx
t3  = t1 * t2
t7  = t6 * dx
y1  = y + t2
c   = x1 < a
t4  = u - t3
u1  = t4 - t7
```

The data-flow graph corresponding to the resulting code above is shown in Figure 3.8. Note that t5 has been relabeled t12 and that t9 has been relabeled t13 to be consistent with the labeling of Figure 3.8.

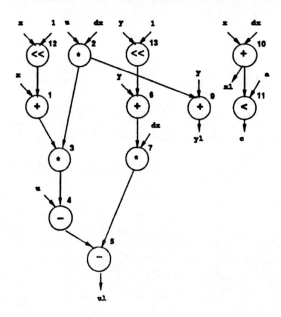

Figure 3.8: Data-flow graph for transformed differential equation code.

Chapter 4

Architectural synthesis

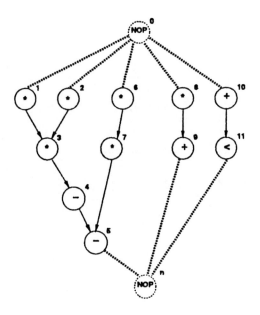

Figure 4.1: Sequencing graph.

4.1

Consider the sequencing graph of Figure 4.1. Assume you have a resource that performs the operations $(+, -, <, *)$ in one cycle and that occupies one unit of area. Determine the area/latency trade-off points. Consider the circuit as resource-dominated with no overhead.

Solution

This can be done by just eye-balling the graph. The area/latency Pareto points are as follows: $(area, latency) = (3, 4), (2, 6), (1, 11)$, as shown in Figure 4.2 (the design evaluation space shown in Figure 4.2 encompasses an area of 5, the maximum number of operations that can be scheduled at once, and a latency of 11, the maximum latency

21

possible). Possible schedules for the points (3.4) and (2.6) are shown in Figures 4.3 and 4.4, respectively. The schedule for (1.11) is trivial. An exact derivation can be achieved using Hu's Theorem (Chapter 5, Theorem 5.4.1). Derivation of Pareto point (3.4) is shown in Example 5.4.4 of the textbook. The derivation of point (2.6) can be done by finding the number of resources required to achieve latency 5, 6, etc. For $\lambda = 5$ the number of resources is $\lceil max(2/2, 4/3, 8/4, 11/5, 12/6) \rceil = 3$ and is not a Pareto point because it is dominated by (3.4). For $\lambda = 6$, the number of resources is $\lceil max(2/3, 4/4, 8/5, 12/6, 13/7) \rceil = 2$. Then $(2,6)$ is a Pareto point. The derivation of $(1, 11)$ is trivial.

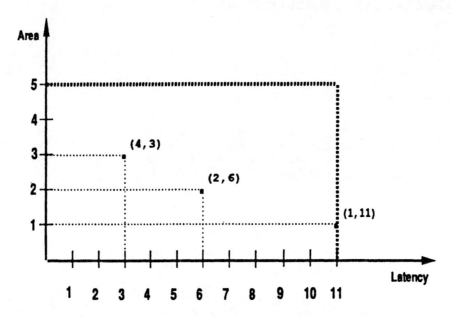

Figure 4.2: Design evaluation space: area/latency trade-off points.

4.2

Consider the sequencing graph of Figure 4.1. Consider a partial binding of operations $\{v_1, v_2\}$ to one resource and $\{v_3, v_6\}$ to another resource. Draw the sequencing graphs that resolve the potential conflicts, including task serialization edges that correspond to this binding. Rank the sequencing graphs in terms of minimum latency. Assume all operations have unit delay.

Solution

The possible solutions for the first binding are executing v_1 before v_2 and executing v_2 before v_1. Similarly, for the second binding the possible solutions are executing v_3 before v_6 and executing v_6 before v_3. Thus 4 relative orderings of the operations are possible (an ordering may have several possible schedules with the same latency), with the relative ordering of executing v_3 before v_6 causing an increase in the latency. Two possible schedules of the two relative orderings of operations v_3 and v_6 are shown in Figure 4.5. The other two relative orderings would be similar, but with v_1 interchanged with v_2. The sequencing graphs with v_6 before v_3 are ranked higher than those with v_3 before v_6 due to the lower latency.

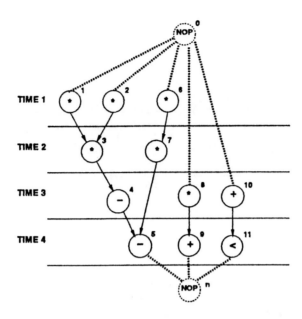

Figure 4.3: One possible sequencing graph for area/latency trade-off point (3, 4).

4.3

Consider the loop of the differential equation integrator. Assume a word length of 8 bits in the data-path. Consider the binding shown in Figure 4.5 (of the textbook). Perform connectivity synthesis and show a diagram with the detailed interconnection among the building blocks of the data-path. Estimate the area, including resources, multiplexers and registers. (Assume that the area of the multiplier and of the ALU are 5 and 1 respectively, the area of a multiplexer is 0.1 unit per input and the area of each register is 0.2 units.)

Solution

Figure 4.5 of the textbook is replicated here as Figure 4.6 for convenience.

For the solution we do not consider the effects of carryouts, overflows, and exceptions.

The solution is found by assigning a register to each of the results needed, overlapping register usage as possible (for example c, although it is a one bit comparison result, is stored in $r4$). The solution is shown in Figure 4.7 and corresponds to the following register assignments:

	Mult1	Mult2	Mult3	Mult4	ALU1	ALU2
time 1:	r1 = 3*x;	r2 = u*dx;	r3 = 3*y;	r4 = u*dx;	x = x+dx;	
time 2:		r2 = r1*r2;	r3 = r3*dx;		r4 = x<a;	y = r4+y;
time 3:						r2 = u-r2;
time 4:						r2 = r2-r3;

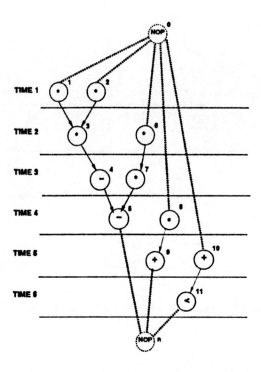

Figure 4.4: Possible sequencing graph for area/latency trade-off point $(2, 6)$.

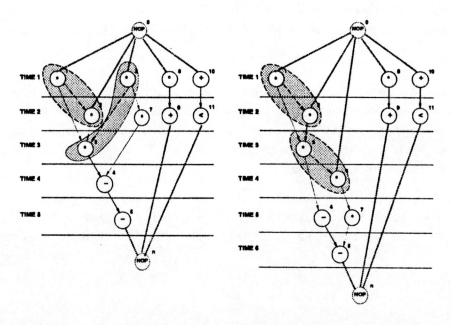

Figure 4.5: Sequencing graphs with v_3 after v_6 and v_3 before v_6. Note that the latency increases.

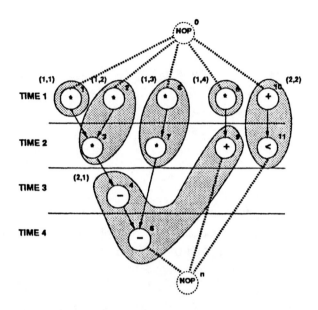

Figure 4.6: Scheduled sequencing graph with resource binding.

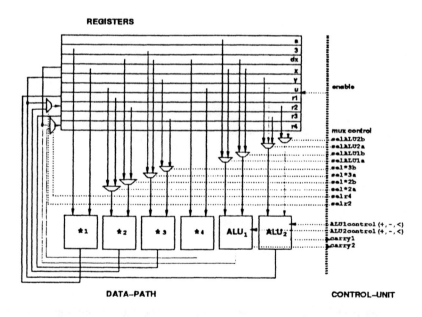

Figure 4.7: Structural view of the differential equation integrator.

The cost of this implementation is as follows:

```
registers:                  .2 * 10 =   2.0
2-input multiplexers:       .2 *  9 =   1.8
3-input multiplexers:       .3 *  1 =   0.3
multipliers:                 4 *  5 =  20.0
ALUs:                        1 *  2 =   2.0
------------------------------------------------
Total                                  26.1
```

4.4

Consider the full example of the differential equation integrator. Assume a word length of 8 bits in the data-path. Consider an implementation with one multiplier and one ALU. Complete the connectivity synthesis, sketched in Figure 4.12, by showing all connections in detail. Construct the state diagram of a finite-state machine controller for the circuit.

Solution

First we need a schedule for an implementation with one multiplier and one ALU. This is shown in Figure 4.8.

The resulting register flow is given in the following table, with definitions of columns as given. This table is included to clarify how the register usage is overlapped in the execution of the operations.

```
Ma = input a of Multiplier
Mb = input b of Multiplier
Mout = output of Multiplier
ALUa = input a of ALU
ALUb = input b of ALU
ALUout = output of ALU
```

State	Ma	Mb	Mout	ALUa	ALUb	ALUout
s2	3	x	r1	dx	x	x
s3	u	dx	r2	a	x	c
s4	r1	r2	r1			
s5	3	y	r1	r1	u	r2
s6	r1	dx	r1			
s7	u	dx	r1	r1	r2	u
s8				r1	y	y

Note that there are 9 states overall; only 7 are used in the loop and they correspond to the schedule steps. (Figure 4.9.)

The result of the multiply operation corresponding to t_1 is stored in the register for x since x is not needed later in the computation. Also note that c is a one bit register which is calculated in time step 2 but is needed at the

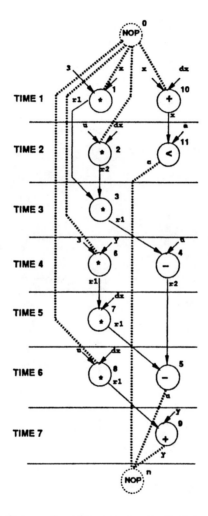

Figure 4.8: Scheduled sequencing graph under resource constraints, annotated with variable flow.

end if the loop to test if we continue looping or not. Finally, note that y and u are also loaded up with the correct values for the next iteration after states 7 and 8.

As shown explicitly in the state diagram in Figure 4.9, all states output the correct bit values to specify the correct register inputs from the multiplexers feeding the multiplier and ALU inputs. The control signals used are selMa[0:1], selMb[0:1], selALUa, and selALUb[0:2], and select registers according to the following table.

selMa[0:1]		selMb[0:1]		selALUa		selALUb[0:2]	
00	3	00	x	0	x	000	dx
01	u	01	dx	1	r1	001	a
10	r1	10	r2			010	u
11	–	11	y			011	r2
						100	y

The enable signals controlling the writing of results and selection of registers are set in the transition between states. The state transition diagram of the control unit is shown in Figure 4.9.

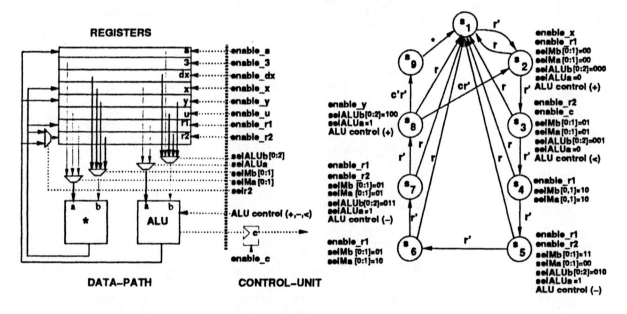

Figure 4.9: Structural view of the differential equation integrator.

4.5

Consider a data-path modeled by the following assignments:

a = i + j; b = k + 1; c = a + b; d = b + n; e = c + m; f = c + e;

The only available resource-type is a 2-input adder. Its delay is 50 nsec. Ignore overflow problems and assume that the input carry is unused. Apply operation chaining when possible.

Consider the circuit as resource-dominated. Determine a minimum-latency schedule for 100 nsec cycle-time, with the reduction of resource usage as a secondary goal. Determine then a minimum-latency schedule with two resources. Draw the corresponding data-path showing the resources, registers and multiplexers.

Assuming that multiplexers have 10 nsec delay, reschedule the operations to meet the cycle-time constraint.

Solution

This problem can be broken down into three questions:

(a) Consider the circuit as resource-dominated. Determine a minimum-latency schedule for 100 nsec cycle-time, with the reduction of resource usage as a secondary goal.

The solution to this can be done in a minimum latency of 2 cycles. First we draw the data-flow graph corresponding to the assignments, shown in Figure 4.10.

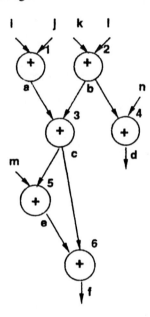

Figure 4.10: Data-flow graph for problem 5.

Next we schedule the operations. Using chaining, only three adders are needed to perform the operations in two cycles. This schedule is shown in Figure 4.11.

(b) Next determine a minimum-latency schedule with two resources. Draw the corresponding data-path showing the resources, registers and multiplexers.

There are many possible solutions to this. Note that no schedule with two steps and two resources is possible, because operations assigned to the same resource cannot be chained in the same control step. One schedule which attains the minimum latency of 3 cycles is shown in Figure 4.12. The data-path corresponding to assigning operations v_1, v_3, and v_5 to one adder and operations v_2, v_4, and v_6 to another adder is shown in Figure 4.13. Note that operations v_5 and v_6 are chained: the output of v_5 goes directly to v_6 without going through an intermediate register.

(c) Assuming that multiplexers have 10 nsec delay, reschedule the operations to meet the cycle-time constraint.

Now that each mux has a 10 nsec delay, we look at the critical register to register delay in Figure 4.12. Assuming that data is multiplexed in before each operation, the critical delay is through a mux to operation v_5 through another

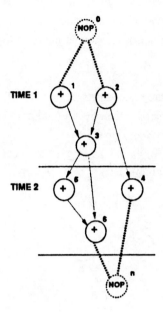

Figure 4.11: Sequencing graph for part (a) of problem 5.

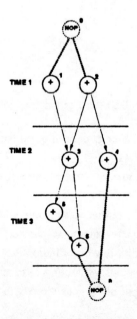

Figure 4.12: Sequencing graph for part (b) of problem 5.

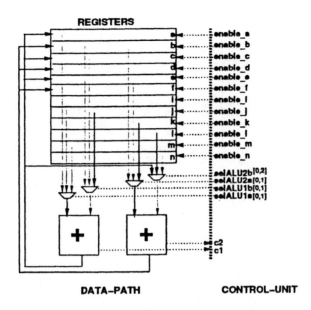

Figure 4.13: Data-path for part (b) of problem 5.

mux to operation v_6; this path yields a total delay of 120nsec. Since this is greater than the cycle time of 100nsec, the schedule in part (b) will not work. To solve this problem, we reschedule operation v_6 in Figure 4.12 to occur one time step later. This removes the chaining and solves the problem at the expense of one cycle, increasing the minimum latency schedule to 4 cycles.

4.6

Consider the following set of scheduled operations:

```
t1:    o1 o6 o10
t2:    o2 o9
t3:    o1 o8
t4:    o3 o5
t5:    o4
t6:    o2 o8
t7:    o7 o9
t8:    o1 o10
t9:    o7 o8
t10:   o9
t11:   o5
```

Draw the operation conflict graph and outline a minimum vertex coloring.

Derive the personality matrix of a microcode ROM for a corresponding control-unit. Use an encoding scheme for the activation signals of the operations that preserves operation concurrency while reducing its width. Minimize the number of decoders. Report the encoding of the signals and the ROM.

Solution

The operation conflict graph is shown in Figure 4.14.

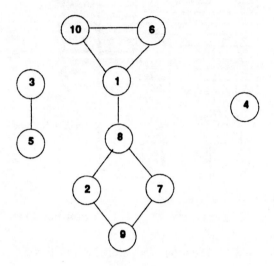

Figure 4.14: Operation conflict graph for problem 6.

A minimum vertex coloring on the operation conflict graph is shown in Figure 4.15.

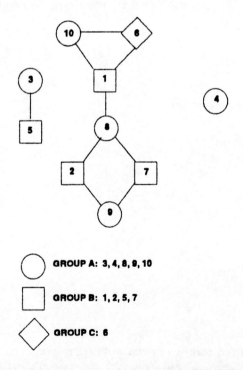

Figure 4.15: Minimum vertex coloring of operation conflict graph.

An encoding for the coloring is as follows:

```
GROUP  A       GROUP  B
Op.  Code      Op.  Code
---  ----      ---  ----

NOP  000       NOP  000
  3  001         1  001
  4  010         2  010
  8  011         5  011
  9  100         7  100
 10  101
```

Note that GROUP C needs no encoding since it is only one bit. This reduces the number of decoders needed to two. The corresponding ROM encoding is as follows:

```
Time  A    B    C
----  ---  ---  -
t1    101  001  1
t2    100  010  0
t3    011  001  0
t4    001  011  0
t5    010  000  0
t6    011  010  0
t7    100  100  0
t8    101  001  0
t9    011  100  0
t10   100  000  0
t11   000  011  0
```

Note that the ROM previous state and next state is assumed (i.e. not explicitly shown).

4.7

Consider the full differential equation integrator. Assume that the ALU executes in one cycle and that the multiplier uses an iterative algorithm with data-dependent delay. A completion signal is provided by the multiplier. Assume dedicated resources. Draw a diagram showing an implementation of the control-unit using the adaptive scheme, and derive a set of logic equations specifying the controller.

Solution

First we draw the sequencing graph corresponding the operations needed for the control-unit implementation and label the nodes. This is shown in Figure 4.16. We assume dedicated resources. All vertices are labeled with double indices $x.y$. The former (i.e., x) is 1 for the root entity and 2 for the loop. The latter index (i.e., y) denotes the operations.

In the control unit implementation we use the following notation. Signal $act\_x.y$ stands for activation and $cn\_x.y$ for completion of operation $x.y$. The latter signal are provided by the individual resources executing the

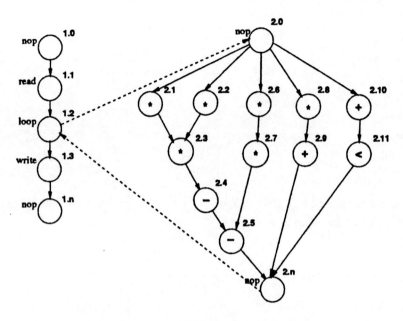

Figure 4.16: Data-flow graph for problem 7.

operation. Each atomic finite-state machine has one bit encoding the state called $state\_x.y$, which is 0 for the *ready* state and 1 for the *wait* state of operation $x.y$.

Thus, the state and output transitions for all non-degenerate atomic finite-state machines are:

$$state\_x.y = (old\_state\_x.y + completion\_x.y) \cdot (done\_x.n + reset)'$$
$$act\_x.y = state\_x.y' \cdot enable\_x.y$$
$$done\_x.y = state\_x.y + state\_x.y \cdot cn\_x.y$$

The first operation is always enabled (i.e., $enable1.0 = 1$). Thus the circuit is started by pulsing the *reset* line that issues signals $r1$ and $r2$ to all atomic finite-state machines. The adaptive implementation is sketched in Figure 4.17. The remaining logic equations are listed next. Note that signal c is provided by the data path.

Root entity:

$$
\begin{aligned}
enable\_1.0 &= 1 \\
done\_1.0 &= enable\_1.0 \\
enable\_1.1 &= done\_1.0 \\
enable\_1.2 &= done\_1.1 \\
cn\_1.2 &= c \cdot done\_2.n \\
enable\_1.3 &= done\_1.2 \\
enable\_1.n &= done\_1.3 \\
done\_1.n &= enable\_1.n \\
r\_1 &= done\_1.n + reset
\end{aligned}
$$

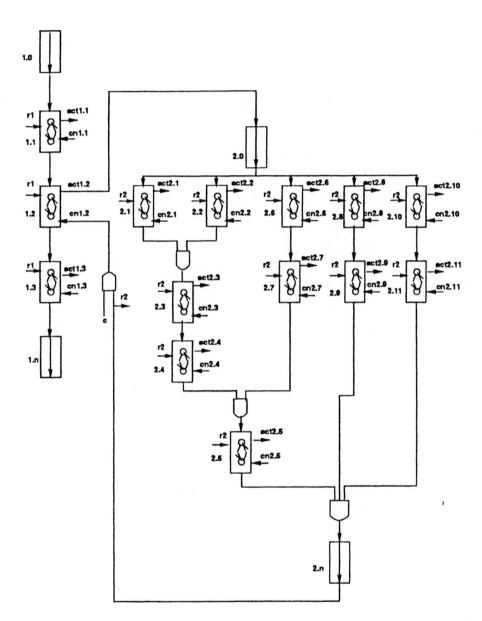

Figure 4.17: Implementation of control-unit using the adaptive scheme.

Loop entity:

$$enable\_2.0 = act\_1.2$$
$$done\_2.0 = enable\_2.0$$
$$enable\_2.1 = done\_2.0$$
$$enable\_2.2 = done\_2.0$$
$$enable\_2.6 = done\_2.0$$
$$enable\_2.8 = done\_2.0$$
$$enable\_2.10 = done\_2.0$$
$$enable\_2.3 = done\_2.1 \cdot done\_2.2$$
$$enable\_2.7 = done\_2.6$$
$$enable\_2.9 = done\_2.8$$
$$enable\_2.11 = done\_2.10$$
$$enable\_2.4 = done\_2.3$$
$$enable\_2.5 = done\_2.4 \cdot done\_2.7$$
$$enable\_2.n = done\_2.5 \cdot done\_2.9 \cdot done\_2.11$$
$$r\_2 = done\_2_n + reset$$

4.8

Consider the full differential equation integrator. Assume that the ALU executes in one cycle and that the multiplier uses an iterative algorithm with data-dependent delay. A completion signal is provided by the multiplier. Assume one multiplier and one ALU are used. Draw the state diagram of the finite-state machine implementing the control-unit.

Solution

For this problem, we use the sequencing graph of Figure 4.8. We call *mdone* the completion signal of the multiplier. The control signal for the registers ar defined as for Problem 4.4. Namely signals selMa[0:1], selMb[0:1], selALUa, and selALUb[0:2] select registers according to the following table.

```
selMa[0:1]  selMb[0:1]  selALUa  selALUb[0:2]
----------  ----------  -------  ------------
00     3    00     x    0    x   000     dx
01     u    01     dx   1    r1  001     a
10     r1   10     r2                010     u
11     -    11     y                 011     r2
                                     100     y
```

The state transition diagram of the control unit is shown in Figure 4.18 below. The enable signals controlling the writing of results and selection of register inputs are set in the transition between states.

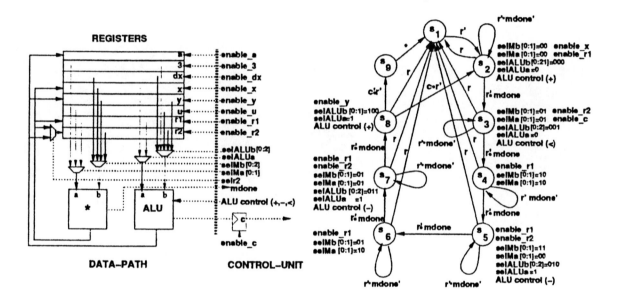

Figure 4.18: Data path and state-transition diagram of the control unit for Problem 4.8.

Chapter 5

Scheduling algorithms

5.1

Consider the graph of Figure 5.1. Assume the execution delays of the multiplier and of the ALU are 2 and 1 cycle respectively. Schedule the graph using the ASAP algorithm. Assuming a latency bound of $\overline{\lambda} = 8$ cycles, schedule the graph using the ALAP algorithm. Determine the mobility of the operations.

Solution

The ASAP schedule is shown in Figure 5.1. Note that the schedule requires a latency of $\lambda = 6$ steps, which is less than the bound.

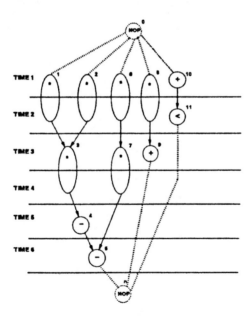

Figure 5.1: ASAP schedule for Figure 5.1.

The ALAP schedule is shown in Figure 5.2.

39

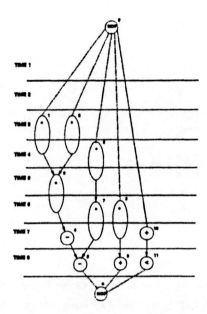

Figure 5.2: ALAP schedule for Figure 5.1 with 8 cycle latency bound.

The following table summarizes the start times in the ASAP schedule, the start times in the ALAP schedule, and mobility.

Operation	ASAP time	ALAP time	Mobility
1	1	3	2
2	1	3	2
3	3	5	2
4	5	7	2
5	6	8	2
6	1	4	3
7	3	6	3
8	1	6	5
9	3	8	5
10	1	7	6
11	2	8	6

5.2

Consider the graph of Figure 5.1. Assume the execution delays of the multiplier and of the ALU are 2 and 1 cycle respectively. Considering the following timing constraints between the start times of the operations:

- Operation v_6 starts at least one cycle after v_4 starts.

- Operations v_5 and v_9 start simultaneously.

- Operation v_9 starts at most 2 cycles after operation v_{10} starts.

Construct a constraint graph. Schedule the operations by assuming that $t_0 = 1$.

Solution

The constraint graph is shown in Figure 5.3. There are two feedback edges labeled (a) and (b) respectively.

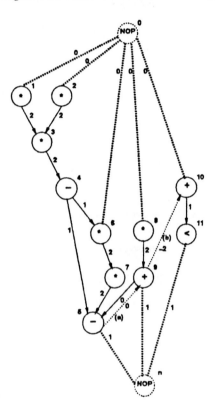

Figure 5.3: Constraint graph for Problem 2.

We use the Liao-Wong algorithm to schedule the operations. First of all we note that $F = 2$, i.e. there are 2 feedback edges. At the first iteration, the longest paths from the source in $G(V, E, W_E)$ are $l_1^2 = 0; l_2^2 = 0; l_3^2 = 2; l_4^2 = 4; l_5^2 = 9; l_6^2 = 5; l_7^2 = 7; l_8^2 = 0; l_9^2 = 2; l_{10}^2 = 0; l_{11}^2 = 1; l_n^2 = 10$. When the algorithm examines the feedback edges, it finds a constraint violation on edge (a): (v_5, v_9). The violation is that $l_9^2 = 2 < l_5^2 + w_{59} = 9 + 0 = 9$. Thus, the algorithm adds edge (t_0, v_9) to E with weight $w_{0,9} = l_5^2 + w_{59} = 9 + 0 = 9$.

At the second iteration the longest paths from the source in $G(V, E, W_E)$ are $l_1^3 = 0; l_2^3 = 0; l_3^3 = 2; l_4^3 = 4; l_5^3 = 9; l_6^3 = 5; l_7^3 = 7; l_8^3 = 0; l_9^3 = 9; l_{10}^3 = 0; l_{11}^3 = 1; l_n^3 = 10$. Only v_9 has changed. When the algorithm examines the feedback edges, it finds a constraint violation on edge (b): (v_9, v_{10}). The violation is that $l_{10}^3 = 0 < l_9^3 + w_{9,10} = 9 - 2 = 7$. Thus, the algorithm adds edge (t_0, v_{10}) to E with weight $w_{0\,10} = l_9^3 + w_{59} = 9 - 2 = 7$.

At the third iteration the longest paths from the source in $G(V, E, W_E)$ are $l_1^3 = 0; l_2^3 = 0; l_3^3 = 2; l_4^3 = 4; l_5^3 = 9; l_6^3 = 5; l_7^3 = 7; l_8^3 = 0; l_9^3 = 9; l_{10}^3 = 7; l_{11}^3 = 8; l_n^3 = 10$. So v_{10} and v_{11} changed.

When the algorithm examines the feedback edges, it does not find any constraint violations and thus terminates successfully.

Now, since we are given that v_0 starts at time 1, the scheduled times for the vertices are one plus their longest paths: $t_1 = 1; t_2 = 1; t_3 = 3; t_4 = 5; t_5 = 10; t_6 = 6; t_7 = 8; t_8 = 1; t_9 = 10; t_{10} = 8; t_{11} = 9; t_n = 11$.

5.3

Consider operations $v_i; i = 1, 2, \ldots, 7$, with the corresponding execution delays: $D = \{0, 1, 3, 1, 1, 1, 4\}$. Assume the following dependencies: $E = \{(v_1, v_2), (v_2, v_3), (v_5, v_6)\}$ and the following constraints:

- Operation v_1 has release time 1.

- Operation v_5 has release time 4.

- Operation v_7 has release time 8.

- Operation v_4 starts at least (no sooner than) four cycles after operation v_2 starts.

- Operation v_4 starts at most one cycle after operation v_3 starts.

- Operation v_7 starts at most two cycles after operation v_6 starts.

- Operation v_5 starts exactly two cycles after operation v_1 starts.

Construct a constraint graph. Schedule the operations by assuming that $t_0 = 1$ with the Liao-Wong algorithm. Show all steps.

Solution

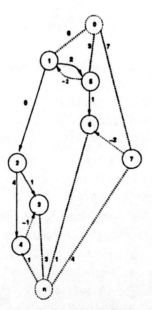

Figure 5.4: Constraint graph for Problem 3.

The constraint graph is shown in Figure 5.4. In particular, it shows the release times (defined in Chapter 2) as weights on edges from the source node (v_0). (Note that the source node starts at time $t_0 = 1$ and so, for example, a release time of one for v_1 translates into an edge of weight zero between (v_0) and (v_1), etc.)

To use the Liao-Wong algorithm, we first determine the set $F = \{(v_5, v_1), (v_7, v_6), (v_4, v_3)\}$ of feedback edges. We compute then the longest paths to each vertex in the dag induced by the remaining edges.

At the first iteration, the longest paths from the source in $G(V, E, W_E)$ are: $l_1^2 = 0; l_2^2 = 0; l_3^2 = 1; l_4^2 = 4; l_5^2 = 3; l_6^2 = 4; l_7^2 = 7; l_n^2 = 11$. When the algorithm examines the feedback edges, it finds constraint violations on all feedback edges. Namely the violations are: $l_1^2 = 0 < l_5^2 + w_{5,1} = 3 - 2 = 1$, $l_3^2 = 1 < l_4^2 + w_{4,3} = 4 - 1 = 3$, and $l_6^2 = 4 < l_7^2 + w_{7,6} = 7 - 2 = 5$. Thus, the algorithm adds edges (v_0, v_1), (v_0, v_3) and (v_0, v_6) to E with weights: $w_{0,1} = l_5^2 + w_{5,1} = 3 - 2 = 1$, $w_{0,3} = l_4^2 + w_{4,3} = 4 - 1 = 3$, and $w_{0,6} = l_7^2 + w_{7,6} = 7 - 2 = 5$.

At the second iteration the longest paths from the source in $G(V, E, W_E)$ are $l_1^3 = 1; l_2^3 = 1; l_3^3 = 3; l_4^3 = 5; l_5^3 = 3; l_6^3 = 5; l_7^3 = 7; l_n^3 = 11$.

When the algorithm examines the feedback edges, it finds the following violation on edge (v_4, v_3): $l_3^3 = 3 < l_4^3 + w_{4,3} = 5 - 1 = 4$. Therefore, the algorithm adds edges (v_0, v_3), with weight: $w_{0,3} = l_4^3 + w_{4,3} = 5 - 1 = 4$.

At the third iteration the longest paths from the source in $G(V, E, W_E)$ are $l_1^4 = 1; l_2^4 = 1; l_3^4 = 4; l_4^4 = 5; l_5^4 = 3; l_6^4 = 5; l_7^4 = 7; l_n^4 = 11$. There are no constraint violations.

Now, since we are given that v_0 starts at time 1, the scheduled times for the vertices are one plus their longest paths: $t_1 = 2; t_2 = 2; t_3 = 5; t_4 = 6; t_5 = 4; t_6 = 6; t_7 = 8; t_n = 12$.

5.4

Let $\widetilde{G}_c(V, E)$ be the subgraph of $G_c(V_c, E_c)$ after having removed all edges corresponding to maximum timing constraints. Assume $\widetilde{G}_c(V, E)$ is acyclic and assume $G_c(V_c, E_c)$ is feasible. Let the anchor set $A(v_i) \subseteq A$ of a vertex $v_i \in V$ be the subset of A such that $a \in A(v_i)$ if there is a path in $\widetilde{G}_c(V, E)$ from a to v_i with an edge weighted by d_a.

Prove that a feasible maximum timing constraint u_{ij} is well-posed (i.e.satisfiable for any value of the anchor delays), if and only if $A(v_j) \subseteq A(v_i)$.

Solution

We use the following notations: $\delta(a)$ is the delay of a, i.e. equal to d_a in the book. The start times of an operations v_i with respect to a is called the offset and is represented as $\sigma_a(v_i)$. Also we denote $\widetilde{G}_c(V, E)$ by $G(V, E_f)$.

In this problem we are asked to prove the following theorem:

Theorem 5A *Let $G(V, E_f)$ be acyclic. A feasible maximum timing constraint $u_{ij} \geq 0$ is well-posed if and only if $A(v_j) \subseteq A(v_i)$.*

Proof: We prove first the necessary condition. For the sake of contradiction, assume $A(v_j)$ is not a subset of $A(v_i)$ and the maximum timing constraint u_{ij} is well-posed. The start time of v_j is $T(v_j) = \max_{a \in A(v_j)} \{T(a) + \delta(a) + \sigma_a(v_j)\}$, and the start time of v_i is $T(v_i) = \max_{a \in A(v_i)} \{T(a) + \delta(a) + \sigma_a(v_i)\}$. The maximum timing constraint implies the condition $T(v_j) \leq T(v_i) + u_{ij}$. The inequality can be written as:

$$T(v_j) - T(v_i) \leq u_{ij}$$
$$\max_{a \in A(v_j)} \{T(a) + \delta(a) + \sigma_a(v_j)\} - \max_{a \in A(v_i)} \{T(a) + \delta(a) + \sigma_a(v_i)\} \leq u_{ij}$$

Since $A(v_j)$ is not a subset of $A(v_i)$, there exists an anchor b such that $b \in A(v_j)$ but $b \notin A(v_i)$. Thus it is always possible to find a value of $\delta(b)$ such that the inequality is violated. Hence, the constraint graph is ill-posed.

We now prove the sufficient condition. If the anchor sets of v_i and v_j for a feasible maximum timing constraint u_{ij} satisfy the condition $A(v_j) \subseteq A(v_i)$, then the constraint implies the following inequality:

$$
\begin{aligned}
T(v_j) &\leq T(v_i) + u_{ij} \\
\max_{a \in A(v_j)} \{T(a) + \delta(a) + \sigma_a(v_j)\} &\leq \max_{a \in A(v_i)} \{T(a) + \delta(a) + \sigma_a(v_i)\} + u_{ij} \\
\max_{a \in A(v_j)} \{T(a) + \delta(a) + \sigma_a(v_j)\} &\leq \max_{a \in A(v_i)} \{T(a) + \delta(a) + (\sigma_a(v_i) + u_{ij})\} \\
\max_{a \in A(v_j)} \{T(a) + \delta(a) + \sigma_a(v_j)\} &\leq \max\{ \max_{a \in A(v_j)} \{T(a) + \delta(a) + (\sigma_a(v_i) + u_{ij})\} \\
& \qquad \max_{x \in A(v_i), x \notin A(v_j)} \{T(x) + \delta(x) + (\sigma_x(v_i) + u_{ij})\}\} \\
\max_{a \in A(v_j)} \{T(a) + \delta(a) + \sigma_a(v_j)\} &\leq \max\{\mathcal{A}, \mathcal{B}\}
\end{aligned}
$$

where we define $\mathcal{A} \equiv \max_{a \in A(v_j)} \{T(a)+\delta(a)+(\sigma_a(v_i)+u_{ij})\}$, and $\mathcal{B} \equiv \max_{x \in A(v_i), x \notin A(v_j)} \{T(x)+\delta(x)+(\sigma_x(v_i)+u_{ij})\}$. It is sufficient to verify that $\max_{a \in A(v_j)}\{T(a)+\delta(a)+\sigma_a(v_j)\} \leq \mathcal{A}$, because $\max_{a \in A(v_j)}\{T(a)+\delta(a)+\sigma_a(v_j)\} \leq \mathcal{A}$ implies $\max_{a \in A(v_j)}\{T(a) + \delta(a) + \sigma_a(v_j)\} \leq \max\{\mathcal{A}, \mathcal{B}\}$. Therefore,

$$
\begin{aligned}
\max_{a \in A(v_j)} \{T(a) + \delta(a) + \sigma_a(v_j)\} &\leq \mathcal{A} \\
\max_{a \in A(v_j)} \{T(a) + \delta(a) + \sigma_a(v_j)\} &\leq \max_{a \in A(v_j)} \{T(a) + \delta(a) + (\sigma_a(v_i) + u_{ij})\}
\end{aligned}
$$

Note that all quantities in the inequality above are non-negative. Since both the left hand and right hand side of the inequality refer to the same set of anchors, determining whether it can be satisfied can be stated in terms of the individual anchors. In particular, for all anchors $a \in A(v_j)$, the following inequality is checked.

$$
\begin{aligned}
T(a) + \delta(a) + \sigma_a(v_j) &\leq T(a) + \delta(a) + (\sigma_a(v_i) + u_{ij}) \\
\sigma_a(v_j) &\leq \sigma_a(v_i) + u_{ij}
\end{aligned}
$$

By the definition of feasible timing constraints, the inequality holds for all offsets $\sigma_a(v_i), v_i \in V$ and anchors $a \in A(v_j)$. Therefore, the maximum timing constraint u_{ij} is satisfied. $\|$.

5.5

Using the definition of Problem 5.4, show that in a well-posed constraint graph the anchor sets on a cycle are identical.

Solution

We want to demonstrate the following theorem:

Theorem 5B *Given a well-posed constraint graph $G(V, E)$, the anchor sets of the vertices on a cycle of G are identical.*

Proof: Let a cycle be formed in the graph by the edges $(v_1, v_2)(v_2, v_3) \cdots (v_{s-1}, v_s)(v_s, v_1)$. The edges can be classified either as *forward* or *backward*. We consider each case separately. If (v_{k-1}, v_k) is a backward edge, then $A(v_{k-1}) \subseteq A(v_k)$ by Theorem 5A because of the well-posedness property. If (v_{k-1}, v_k) is a forward edge, then from the definition of anchor sets, $A(v_{k-1}) \subseteq A(v_k)$ because v_{k-1} is the predecessor of v_k. Combining the two requirements, the edges in the cycle imply that,

$$A(v_1) \subseteq A(v_2) \subseteq \cdots \subseteq A(v_s) \subseteq A(v_1)$$

which can be true if and only if the anchor sets are identical,

$$A(v_1) \equiv A(v_1) \equiv \cdots \equiv A(v_s)$$

for all cycles in the graph. ||

Since two cycles in the graph with a common vertex is also a cycle, the anchor sets for the vertices on all connected cycles are identical.

5.6

Using the definition of Problem 5.4, show that in a well-posed constraint graph the weight of any cycle is bounded.

Solution

Stated another way, we want to prove the following theorem:

Theorem 5C *Given a well-posed constraint graph $G(V, E)$, no cycles with unbounded length exist in G.*

Proof: We will prove by contradiction. Assume G is well-posed but there exists a cycle with unbounded length. Let the cycle be denoted by C. Since C has unbounded length, this implies that there exists an anchor a on the cycle such that the length of the cycle is greater than or equal to the execution delay $\delta(a)$. Consider now the next vertex v that follows a on the cycle C. By definition of anchor sets, a is in the anchor set of v, i.e. $a \in A(v)$. From Theorem 5B, the anchor sets of all vertices on the cycle must be identical, implying that a is also in the anchor set of a itself. This results in a contradiction. Therefore, we conclude that no cycle of unbounded length exists in G. ||

5.7

Under the definitions and assumptions of Problem 5.4, show that a constraint graph is well-posed if and only if $R(v_i) \subseteq A(v_i) \; \forall v_i \in V$.

Solution

We prove this in two steps. First, using Theorem 5A, we state the following key theorem:

Theorem 5D *Let $G(V, E_f)$ be acyclic. A feasible constraint graph $G(V, E)$ is well-posed if and only if $A(v_i) \subseteq A(v_j)$ for all edges $\epsilon_{ij} \in E$.*

Proof: First we prove the necessary condition by induction. We will show that a given well-posed constraint graph, if an edge ϵ_{ij} is added such that $A(v_i) \subseteq A(v_j)$, then the resulting graph is well-posed also. Initially, consider the graph consisting of forward edges E_f only. Since $G(V, E_f)$ is acyclic and by the definition of anchor sets the condition holds, and $G(V, E_f)$ is well-posed. Now consider a backward edge $\epsilon_{ij} \in E_b$ representing a feasible maximum timing constraint u_{ji}, where by assumption $A(v_i) \subseteq A(v_j)$. From Theorem 5A, u_{ji} is well-posed if and only if $A(v_i) \subseteq A(v_j)$. Therefore, the resulting graph is well-posed also, and the induction is complete.

Now we prove the sufficient condition. Assume $G(V, E)$ is well-posed and there exist an edge $\epsilon_{ij} \in E$ for which $A(v_i)$ is not a subset of $A(v_j)$. By definition of anchor sets, ϵ_{ij} cannot be a forward edge, and hence ϵ_{ij} must be a backward edge that is derived from a feasible maximum timing constraint. Since all constraints implied by G are well-posed, it follows from Theorem 5A that $A(v_i) \subseteq A(v_j)$. This results in a contradiction. Therefore, the criterion $A(v_i) \subseteq A(v_j)$ must be satisfied for all edges in the graph. $\|$

Now we prove what we were asked to, namely the following theorem:

Theorem 5E *Let $G(V, E_f)$ be acyclic. A feasible constraint graph $G(V, E)$ is well-posed if and only if $R(v_i) \subseteq A(v_i)$ for all $v_i \in V$.*

Proof: From Theorem 5D, it is sufficient to show that $R(v_i) \subseteq A(v_i) \; \forall v_i \in V$ implies $A(v_i) \subseteq A(v_j)$ $\forall \epsilon_{ij} \in E$, and vice versa. We prove the sufficient condition first. Assume that $A(v_i) \subseteq A(v_j)$ for all $\epsilon_{ij} \in E$. Consider a relevant anchor $r \in R(v_i)$ of a vertex $v_i \in V$. By definition, there exists a defining path from r to v_i, denoted by $(r, v_1), (v_1, v_2), \cdots, (v_k, v_i)$, such that r is an anchor and $\{v_1, \cdots, v_k\}$ are not anchors. By assumption of well-posedness, the edges imply that

$$A(v_1) \subseteq A(v_2) \subseteq \cdots \subseteq A(v_k) \subseteq A(v_i)$$

Since $r \in A(v_1)$, this implies that $r \in A(v_i)$ for all relevant anchors $r \in R(v_i)$. Therefore, $R(v_i) \subseteq A(v_i)$.

We prove the necessary condition by contradiction. Assume $R(v_i) \subseteq A(v_i)$ for all $v_i \in V$. Assume also there exists vertices v_i and v_j such that $e'_{ij} \in E$, and the condition $A(v_i) \subseteq A(v_j)$ is violated. Then there exists an anchor x such that $x \in A(v_i)$ and $x \notin A(v_j)$. By the definition of anchor sets, the violating edge e'_{ij} cannot be a forward edge. Since $x \in A(v_i)$, there is a path of forward edges from x to v_i with the unbounded edge weight $\delta(x)$. If the path contains no other unbounded delay edges, then we have a contradiction because x is a relevant anchor of v_j (by the defining path from x to v_i followed by the edge e'_{ij}), but $x \notin A(v_j)$.

Now consider the case when the path contains other unbounded delay edges. In particular, let an anchor q be on the path from x to v_i such that $q \in A(v_i)$. However, q cannot be in the anchor set $A(v_j)$, otherwise we would violate our initial assumption of $x \notin A(v_j)$. By replacing x by q, the same argument can be applied. Therefore, the condition $A(v_i) \subseteq A(v_j)$, $\forall \epsilon_{ij} \in E$ is satisfied, and the graph is well-posed. $\|$

5.8

Consider the sequencing graph of Figure 5.1. Assume that all operations have unit delay. Formulate the ILP constraint inequalities with a latency bound $\overline{\lambda} = 5$. Write the objective function that models latency minimization.

Solution

To solve this, we first need ASAP and ALAP schedules. The ASAP schedule is already shown in the book, in Figure 5.2. The ALAP is shown below in Figure 5.5. Having computed these schedules, we can now formulate the ILP inequalities.

Let us consider the constraint sets one at a time. First, all operations must start only once:

$$x_{0,1} + x_{0,2} = 1$$
$$x_{1,1} + x_{1,2} = 1$$
$$x_{2,1} + x_{2,2} = 1$$

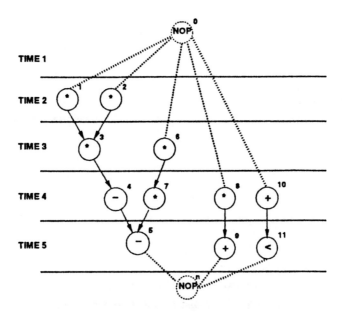

Figure 5.5: ALAP schedule for Problem 8.

$$x_{3,2} + x_{3,3} = 1$$
$$x_{4,3} + x_{4,4} = 1$$
$$x_{5,4} + x_{5,5} = 1$$
$$x_{6,1} + x_{6,2} + x_{6,3} = 1$$
$$x_{7,2} + x_{7,3} + x_{7,4} = 1$$
$$x_{8,1} + x_{8,2} + x_{8,3} + x_{8,4} = 1$$
$$x_{9,2} + x_{9,3} + x_{9,4} + x_{9,5} = 1$$
$$x_{10,1} + x_{10,2} + x_{10,3} + x_{10,4} = 1$$
$$x_{11,2} + x_{11,3} + x_{11,4} + x_{11,5} = 1$$
$$x_{n,5} + x_{n,6} = 1$$

We consider next the constraints based on sequencing:

$$2x_{3,2} + 3x_{3,3} - x_{1,1} - 2x_{1,2} - 1 \geq 0$$
$$2x_{3,2} + 3x_{3,3} - x_{2,1} - 2x_{2,2} - 1 \geq 0$$
$$3x_{4,3} + 4x_{4,4} - 2x_{3,2} - 3x_{3,3} - 1 \geq 0$$
$$4x_{5,4} + 5x_{5,5} - 3x_{4,3} - 4x_{4,4} - 1 \geq 0$$
$$4x_{5,4} + 5x_{5,5} - 2x_{7,2} - 3x_{7,3} - 4x_{7,4} - 1 \geq 0$$
$$2x_{7,2} + 3x_{7,3} + 4x_{7,4} - x_{6,1} - 2x_{6,2} - 3x_{6,3} - 1 \geq 0$$
$$2x_{9,2} + 3x_{9,3} + 4x_{9,4} + 5x_{9,5} - x_{8,1} - 2x_{8,2} - 3x_{8,3} - 4x_{8,4} - 1 \geq 0$$
$$2x_{11,2} + 3x_{11,3} + 4x_{11,4} + 5x_{11,5} - x_{10,1} - 2x_{10,2} - 3x_{10,3} - 4x_{10,4} - 1 \geq 0$$

$$5x_{n.5} + 6x_{n.6} - 4x_{5.4} - 5x_{5.5} - 1 \geq 0$$
$$5x_{n.5} + 6x_{n.6} - 2x_{9.2} - 3x_{9.3} - 4x_{9.4} - 5x_{9.5} - 1 \geq 0$$
$$5x_{n.5} + 6x_{n.6} - 2x_{11.2} - 3x_{11.3} - 4x_{11.4} - 5x_{11.5} - 1 \geq 0$$

No resource constraints are specified.

The objective function is $min(5x_{n.5} + 6x_{n.6})$. Any set of start times satisfying these constraints provides us with a feasible solution.

5.9

Determine the type distributions for the *scheduled* sequencing graph of Figure 5.8.

Solution

The solution is shown in Figure 5.6. In the top part we show a block version of Figure 5.8 (of the textbook) to visualize concurrency. In the bottom part we show the distribution graphs corresponding to the multiply operations (on the left) and the distribution graph corresponding to the ALU operations (on the right).

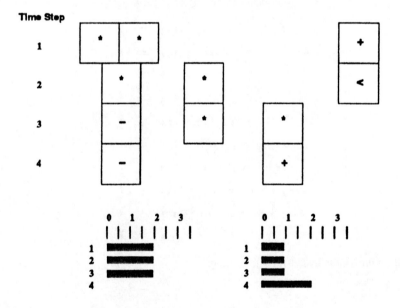

Figure 5.6: Distribution graphs for multiplier and ALU operations of Figure 5.8.

5.10

Explain how you would extend the force-directed scheduling algorithm to handle multi-cycle operations. Describe the extensions to the computation of the time-frames, operation and type probabilities.

Solution

Operations that require multiple cycles can be modeled with two simple extensions to the force-directed scheduling algorithm given in Section 5.4.4.

The first extension has to do with the determination of the time frames. This is done in a straightforward fashion by extending the time frame of a multicycle operation past the last possible cycle in which the operation can begin executions by the number of cycles needed for the operation to complete execution. For example, if a multiply operation takes 2 cycles, and it begins in cycle 3 in an ASAP schedule while beginning in cycle 5 in an ALAP schedule, its time frame spans cycle 3 through cycle 6.

The second extension has to do with the evaluation of operation distributions. The distributions of multi-cycle operations has to be handled differently since each cycle of the operation must be taken into account. For example, if a multiply operation takes 2 cycles and is scheduled to begin in time step 1, its distribution (or probability) is equal to one in both time step 1 and in time step 2. On the other hand, if it can start in time step 1 or 2, the schedule of starting in time step 1 contributes a 1/2 probability to time steps 1 and 2, while the schedule of starting in time step 2 contributes a 1/2 probability to time steps 2 and 3. The combined distribution is thus 1/2, 1, and 1/2 in time step 1, 2, and 3. The value of 1 in time step 2 indicates that one of the two multiply stages must be scheduled in that time step. The operation-type probabilities are computed by summing up the operation probabilities of the given type at each schedule step.

5.11

Write the pseudo-code of a list scheduler for the minimum latency problem under resource and relative timing constraints.

Solution

We report again the algorithm of list scheduling to minimize latency under resource constraints:

```
LIST_L( G_s(V, E) , a ) {
    l = 1;
    repeat {
        for each resource type k = 1.2....n_res {
            Determine candidate operations U_{l,k};
            Determine unfinished operations T_{l,k};
            Select S_k ⊆ U_{l,k} vertices, such that |S_k| + |T_{l,k}| ≤ a_k;
            Schedule the S_k operations at step l by setting t_i = l  ∀i : v_i ∈ S_k;
        }
        l = l + 1;
    }
    until (v_n is scheduled) ;
    return (t);
}
```

Recall that the candidate operations $U_{l,k}$ are those operations of type k whose predecessors have already been scheduled early enough so that the corresponding operations are completed by step l. Namely: $U_{l,k} = \{v_i \in V : T(v_i) = k$ and $t_j + d_j \leq l \quad \forall j : (v_j, v_i) \in E\}$, for any resource type $k = 1.2.\dots.n_{res}$. Also, recall that the unfinished operations $T_{l,k}$ are those operations of type k that started at earlier cycles and whose execution is not finished at step l. Namely: $T_{l,k} = \{v_i \in V : T(v_i) = k$ and $t_i + d_i > l\}$. Obviously, when the execution delays are one, the set of unfinished operations is empty.

Relative timing constraints are modeled by lower and upper bounds, as defined in Section 5.3.3 of the textbook. Lower bounds affect only the set of candidate operations $U_{l,k}$. Namely: $U_{l,k} = \{v_i \in V : T(v_i) = k$ and $t_j + d_j \leq l \quad \forall j : (v_j, v_i) \in E$ and $t_j + l_{ji} \leq l \quad \forall j : l_{ji}$ is a specified minimum timing constraint $\}$.

Upper bounds are taken into account in the selection step. Given $G_s(V, E)$, let $Q \subseteq V$ be those operations whose start time is bounded from above and $\forall v \in Q$ let $Q(v) \subseteq V$ denote the subset of operations whose timing separation from v is bounded from above.

An algorithm for list scheduling to minimize latency under resource and relative timing constraints is as follows:

```
LIST_L_RT( Gₛ(V,E) , a ) {
     l = 1;
     repeat {
          for each resource type k = 1.2....nᵣₑₛ {
               Determine candidate operations U_{l,k};
               Determine unfinished operations T_{l,k};
               for each unscheduled vᵢ ∈ Q {
                    P(vᵢ) = {v ∈ Q(vᵢ) : v has already been scheduled } ;
                    sᵢ =  min   (tⱼ + uⱼᵢ - l);                    /* compute slack */
                        vⱼ∈P(vᵢ)
                    if (sᵢ < 0) return (∅);
               }
               Select Sₖ ⊆ U_{l,k} vertices with minimum slack, such that |Sₖ| + |T_{l,k}| ≤ aₖ;
               Schedule the Sₖ operations at step l by setting tᵢ = l ∀i : vᵢ ∈ Sₖ;
          }
          l = l + 1;
     }
     until (vₙ is scheduled) ;
     return (t);
}
```

The rationale of the algorithm is to first schedule the operations with upper bounds on their start times, to attempt to satisfy all upper bounds. If an upper bound is violated during the construction of the schedule, the algorithm terminates unsuccessfully. Note that the algorithm may not find a feasible schedule when one exists.

5.12

Consider the problem of unconstrained scheduling with chaining. Assume that the propagation delay of the resources is bounded by the cycle-time. Show how to extend the ASAP scheduling algorithm to incorporate chaining.

Solution

We report again the ASAP algorithm:

ASAP ($G_s(V, E)$) {

    Schedule v_0 by setting $t_0^S = 1$;

    repeat {

        Select a vertex v_i whose predecessors are all scheduled;

        Schedule v_i by setting $t_i^S = \max\limits_{j:(v_j, v_i) \in E} t_j^S + d_j$;

    }

    until (v_n is scheduled) ;

    return ($\mathbf{t}^S$);

}

In the following, let d_i be the propagation delay (e.g., in nanoseconds) of operation v_i, let ϕ be the cycle time, and let e_i be the time span from the beginning of the cycle under consideration to the end of execution of operation v_i.

The algorithm has two nested loops. It finds all operations that can be scheduled with chaining in each time step in the inner loop, and then schedules them in the outer loop.

ASAP_CHAIN ($G_s(V, E)$) {

    $l = 1$;

    Schedule v_0 by setting $t_0^S = 1$;

    repeat {

        $e_i = 0$;

        $C = \emptyset$;

        repeat {

            Select an operation v_i such that:

                all its predecessors are either scheduled or in C and

                $\{e_i \equiv \max\limits_{j:(v_j, v_i) \in E} e_j + d_i\} < \phi$;

            $C = C \cup v_i$;

        }

        until (no v_i is selected) ;

        Schedule each operation $v_i \in C$ by setting $t_i^S = l$;

        $l = l + 1$;

    }

    until (v_n is scheduled) ;

    return ($\mathbf{t}^S$);

}

5.13

Consider the ILP formulation for the minimum-latency scheduling problem, under resource constraints and with alternative operations. Assume that the groups of alternative operations do not form a partition of the set V.

Determine an inequality constraint representing resource usage bounds.

Solution

The resource constraints expressed by Inequality 5.7 of the textbook must reflect that alternative operations can be scheduled in the same steps without affecting the resource constraints. Therefore, inequality 5.7 can be restated as follows:

$$\sum_{i:T(v_i)=k} \max_{e \in E(i)} \sum_{m=l-d_e+1}^{l} x_{em} \le a_k \quad k = 1.2,\ldots,n_{res}; \quad l = 1,2,\ldots,\overline{\lambda}+1 \tag{5.1}$$

where the $E(i) \subseteq V$ is the subset of operations that includes v_i and all operations that are mutually exclusive to v_i. The above equation can be transformed into a linear constraint as follows:

$$\sum_{e \in E(i):T(v_e)=k} \sum_{m=l-d_e+1}^{l} x_{em} \le a_k \quad k = 1,2,\ldots,n_{res}; \quad l = 1,2,\ldots,\overline{\lambda}+1; \quad i = 1,2,\ldots,n \tag{5.2}$$

5.14

Consider the ILP formulation for scheduling with pipelined resources. Derive a set of inequality constraints for the case of multi-cycle resources. Apply the inequalities to Example 5.6.3.

Solution

For the sake of simplicity we assume that the data introduction intervals are one. There are three requirements: (1) operations start only once; (2) sequencing dependencies have to be preserved; (3) no more than a_k operations of type $k = 1.2,\ldots,n_{res}$ can start at the same time, to avoid data overlap.

$$
\begin{aligned}
\text{minimize} \quad & \mathbf{c}^T \mathbf{t} \quad \text{such that} \\
\sum_l x_{il} &= 1 \quad i = 0,1,\ldots,n \\
\sum_l l \cdot x_{il} - \sum_l l \cdot x_{jl} - d_j &\ge 0 \quad i,j = 0.1,\ldots,n \; : (v_j,v_i) \in E \\
\sum_{i:T(v_i)=k} x_{il} &\le a_k \quad k = 1.2,\ldots,n_{res}; \quad l = 1.2,\ldots,\overline{\lambda}+1 \\
x_{il} &\in \{0.1\} \quad i = 0.1,\ldots,n. \quad l = 1.2,\ldots,\overline{\lambda}+1
\end{aligned}
$$

Let us consider Example 5.6.3 of the textbook and let us apply the ILP inequalities. Let us assume that $\overline{\lambda} = 6$. Let us consider the constraint sets one at a time. First, all operations must start only once.

$$
\begin{aligned}
x_{0.1} &= 1 \\
x_{1.1} &= 1 \\
x_{2.1} &= 1 \\
x_{3.3} &= 1
\end{aligned}
$$

$$x_{4,5} = 1$$
$$x_{5,6} = 1$$
$$x_{6,1} + x_{6,2} = 1$$
$$x_{7,3} + x_{7,4} = 1$$
$$x_{8,1} + x_{8,2} + x_{8,3} + x_{8,4} = 1$$
$$x_{9,3} + x_{9,4} + x_{9,5} + x_{9,6} = 1$$
$$x_{10,1} + x_{10,2} + x_{10,3} + x_{10,4} + x_{10,5} = 1$$
$$x_{11,2} + x_{11,3} + x_{11,4} + x_{11,5} + x_{11,6} = 1$$
$$x_{n,7} = 1$$

We consider then the constraints based on sequencing. We report here the non-trivial constraints only, i.e. those involving more than one possible start time for at least one operation.

$$3x_{7,3} + 4x_{7,4} - x_{6,1} - 2x_{6,2} - 2 \geq 0$$
$$3x_{9,3} + 4x_{9,4} + 5x_{9,5} + 6x_{9,6} - x_{8,1} - 2x_{8,2} - 3x_{8,3} - 4x_{8,4} - 2 \geq 0$$
$$2x_{11,2} + 3x_{11,3} + 4x_{11,4} + 5x_{11,5} + 6x_{11,6} - x_{10,1} - 2x_{10,2} - 3x_{10,3} - 4x_{11,4} - 5x_{11,5} - 1 \geq 0$$
$$6x_{5,6} - 3x_{7,3} - 4x_{7,4} - 2 \geq 0$$
$$7x_{n,7} - 3x_{9,3} - 4x_{9,4} - 5x_{9,5} - 6x_{9,6} - 1 \geq 0$$
$$7x_{n,7} - 2x_{11,2} - 3x_{11,3} - 4x_{11,4} - 5x_{11,5} - 6x_{11,6} - 1 \geq 0$$

Finally we consider the resource constraints:

$$x_{1,1} + x_{2,1} + x_{6,1} + x_{8,1} \leq 3$$
$$x_{6,2} + x_{8,2} \leq 3$$
$$x_{3,3} + x_{7,3} + x_{8,3} \leq 3$$
$$x_{7,4} + x_{8,4} \leq 3$$
$$x_{10,1} \leq 1$$
$$x_{10,2} + x_{11,2} \leq 1$$
$$x_{9,3} + x_{10,3} + x_{11,3} \leq 1$$
$$x_{9,4} + x_{10,4} + x_{11,4} \leq 1$$
$$x_{4,5} + x_{9,5} + x_{10,5} + x_{11,5} \leq 1$$
$$x_{5,6} + x_{9,6} + x_{11,6} \leq 1$$

5.15

Determine the type distributions for the pipelined *scheduled* sequencing graph of Figure 5.14.

Solution

The solution is shown in Figure 5.7. In the top part we show a block version of Figure 5.14 (of the textbook) to visualize concurrency. In the bottom part we show the distribution graphs corresponding to the multiply operations (on the left) and the distribution graph corresponding to the ALU operations (on the right).

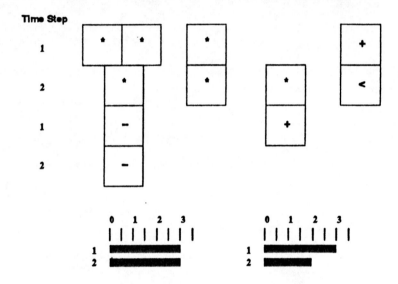

Figure 5.7: Distribution graphs for multiplier and ALU operations of Figure 5.14.

5.16

Consider the sequencing graph of Figure 5.1. Assume that the multiplier and the ALU have execution delays of 2 and 1 cycle respectively. Formulate the ILP constraint inequalities for a pipeline schedule with $\delta_0 = i$.

Solution

To sustain a data introduction interval $\delta = 1$ we need to assume that the multipliers are internally pipelined, even though their delay is 2 units. Thus, the ILP inequalities representing the uniqueness of the start times and the sequencing dependencies are the same as in Problem 5.14. (To limit the size of the inequalities, we assume also $\overline{\lambda} = 6$ and we drop variables that are always zero.)

The requirement of $\delta = 1$ means that all operations must execute concurrently. Thus, resource bounds inequalities are as follows.

For the multiplication operations:

$$x_{1,1} + x_{2,1} + x_{3,3} + x_{6,1} + x_{6,2} + x_{7,3} + x_{7,4} + x_{8,1} + x_{8,2} + x_{8,3} + x_{8,4} \leq a_{mult} \qquad (5.3)$$

For the ALU operations:

$$x_{4,5} + x_{5,6} + x_{9,3} + x_{9,4} + x_{9,5} + x_{9,6} + x_{10,1} + x_{10,2} + + x_{10,3} + x_{10,4} + x_{10,5} + x_{11,2} + x_{11,3} + x_{11,4} + x_{11,5} + x_{11,6} \leq a_{add}$$

$$(5.4)$$

Any set of start times satisfying these constraints provides us with a feasible solution. Note that at least 6 multipliers and 5 ALUs are required.

Chapter 6

Resource sharing and binding

6.1

Draw the compatibility and conflict graphs for the scheduled sequencing graph of Figure 5.2 . Determine an optimum clique partition of the former and a coloring of the latter. How many resources are required for each type?

Solution

The compatibility graphs are show in Figure 6.1, with the compatibility subgraph for multiply operations shown on the left and the compatibility subgraph for ALU operations shown on the right.

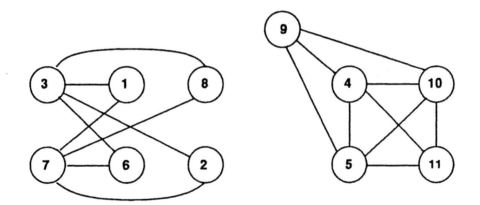

Figure 6.1: Compatibility graph for the sequencing graph of Figure 5.2 of the textbook.

The conflict graphs for the multiplier and ALU types are show in Figure 6.2. An optimal clique partition of the compatibility graphs is shown in Figure 6.3. An optimal vertex coloring of the conflict graph is shown in Figure 6.4. Four multipliers and 2 ALUs are required.

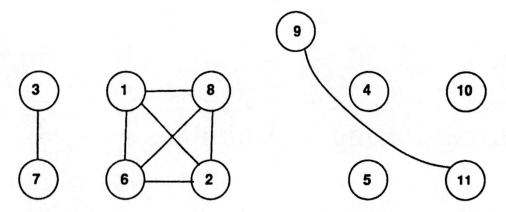

Figure 6.2: Conflict graphs for the multiply and ALU operations of the sequencing graph of Figure 5.2 of the textbook.

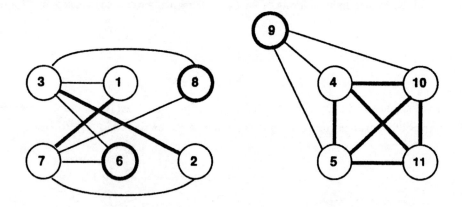

Figure 6.3: Clique partitions of the compatibility graphs of the multiply and ALU operations.

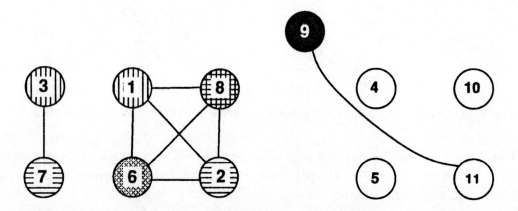

Figure 6.4: Optimal coloring of the conflict graphs for multiply and ALU operations.

6.2

Assume only one resource-type. Determine a property of the conflict graphs related to a non-hierarchical sequencing graphs when all operations have unit execution delay.

Solution

The conflict graph is an interval graph, as shown in Section 6.2.1 of the textbook. In addition, the conflict graph has the property of consisting of (one or more) disjoint cliques, because conflicts are related only to operation concurrency and concurrent operations have exactly the same execution interval because their length is one.

6.3

Consider the register assignment problem of Example 6.2.10. Assume that the intermediate variables are labeled as in Example 6.2.10, and that the inner loop of the differential equation integrator is scheduled as in Figure 4.3. Determine the circular-arc conflict graph of the intermediate and loop variables and a minimum coloring.

Solution

The schedule of Figure 4.3 is repeated in Figure 6.5, along with the new variable lifetimes.

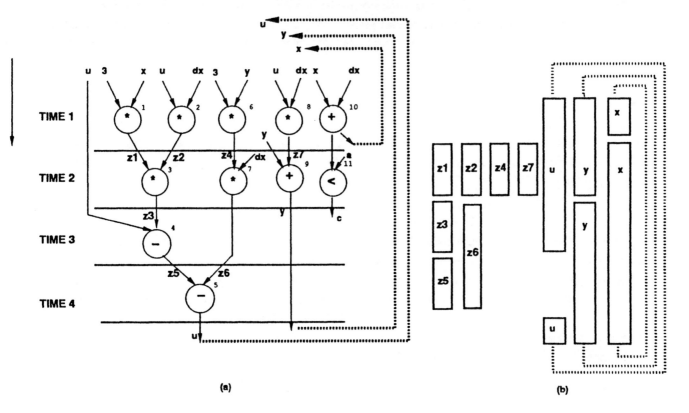

Figure 6.5: (a) Sequencing graph. (b) Variable lifetimes.

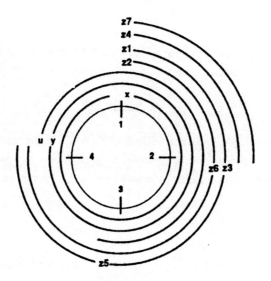

Figure 6.6: Variable lifetimes as arcs in a circle.

Variable lifetimes as arcs in a circle are shown in Figure 6.6.

The circular-arc conflict graph of the intermediate variables and the loop variables is shown in Figure 6.7.

A minimum coloring of the circular-arc conflict graph is shown in Figure 6.8. The coloring requires 7 colors (i.e. registers). Namely: color1 - x; color2 - y; color3 - {u, z5}; color4 - {z1, z3}; color5 - {z6, z7}; color6 - z4; and color7 - z2.

6.4

Consider the unscheduled sequencing graph of Figure 4.2. Assume that we use 2 ALUs and 2 multipliers. Compute how many possible bindings exist of the 6 multiplications, and the overall number of bindings when using two resources per type.

Solution

There are $p(5.2) = 15$ possible bindings for the 2 ALUs, as shown by Example 6.5.5 of the textbook. Let us consider now the 2 multipliers. The possible bindings are $p(6.2)$.

We consider first the number of ways in which the 6 multiplications can be partitioned into 2 blocks. There are $m(6.2) = 5$ ways, as easily determined by Equations 6.11, 6.12 and 6.13. These partitions are as follows: $(1.5).(2.4).(3.3).(4.2).(1.5)$. (The first partition, i.e., (1.5), means that one multiplier implements 1 multiplication and the other multiplier implements 5 multiplications and so on.)

Then $p(6.2)$ is given by Equation 6.18 as follows:

$$p(6.2) = \sum_{i=1}^{5} \left[\frac{\dbinom{n}{m_1^i} \cdot \dbinom{n - m_1^i}{m_2^i} \dots \dbinom{n - \sum_{j=1}^{a-1} m_j^i}{m_a^i}}{a!} \right]$$

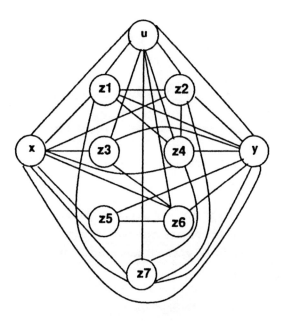

Figure 6.7: Circular-arc conflict graph.

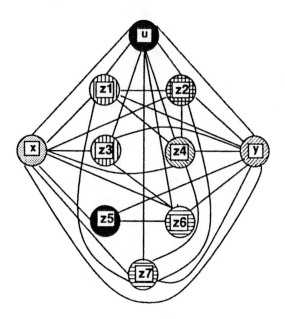

Figure 6.8: Optimally colored circular-arc conflict graph.

where $a = 2$. Therefore:

$$p(6,2) = \frac{1}{2}\left[\binom{6}{1}\cdot\binom{6-1}{5} + \binom{6}{2}\cdot\binom{6-2}{4} + \binom{6}{3}\cdot\binom{6-3}{3} + \binom{6}{4}\cdot\binom{6-4}{2} + \binom{6}{5}\cdot\binom{6-5}{1} \right]$$

$$p(6,2) = \frac{1}{2}\ (6 + 15 + 20 + 15 + 6) = 31$$

When 2 ALUs and 2 multipliers are used, the total number of possible bindings are: $15 * 31 = 465$.

6.5

We consider non-hierarchical sequencing graphs with one resource-type and unbounded delays. Propose a method to determine a bound on the minimum number of resources needed, so that the overall execution delay, for any values of the unbounded delays, is the same as when all resources are dedicated. Extend then the analysis to hierarchical graphs and to multiple resource-types.

Solution

Consider first non-hierarchical sequencing graphs and one resource type. The start times of the operations can vary according to the data-dependent delays, making it difficult to assess the operation concurrency. In any event, operation pairs linked by a path in the graph are not concurrent. In the limiting case that all operations have unbounded delays, such pairs are also the only ones that are not concurrent for any value of the operation delays. Therefore the compatibility graph is the underlying undirected graph of the transitive closure of the sequencing graph (after having deleted the source and sink vertices). Such a graph is a comparability graph because the transitive closure is a transitive orientation of the compatibility graph. Hence, the maximum concurrent resource usage can be computed in polynomial time, by clique partitioning. The concurrency factor is defined to be the clique-cover number of that compatibility graph. When some operations have data-independent delays, then the concurrency factor is an upper bound on the minimum resource requirement, because there may exist start-time assignments to these operations that increase their compatibility.

Let us consider now hierarchical graphs. The concurrency factor can be computed bottom-up. Now vertices in each graph entity are weighted as follows. Each operation vertex has unit weight, each link vertex corresponding to a *model* call or *loop* has a weight corresponding to the concurrency factor of the corresponding graph entity and each link vertex corresponding to a *branching* has a weight equal to the maximum of the concurrency factors of the related graphs. The corresponding hierarchical compatibility graph can be derived by replacing each vertex by as many vertices as its weight. The undirected edge set joins those vertices whose corresponding ones in the sequencing graph are joined by a path. Such a graph is a comparability graph.

Let us consider as an example the sequencing graph of Figure 6.9 (a), where all operations have the same type. The corresponding compatibility graph is shown in Figure 6.9 (b). The concurrency factor is 2.

Let us consider now the sequencing graph of Figure 6.9 (c), with a branch vertex. There is only one body associated with the branch, corresponding to the graph of Figure 6.9 (a). Figure 6.9 (d) shows the vertex weights and Figure 6.9 (e) the compatibility graph related to hierarchical sequencing graph with root shown in Figure 6.9 (c). The overall concurrency factor is 3, that is the clique-cover number.

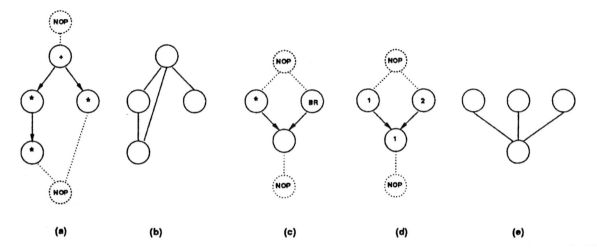

Figure 6.9: (a) Sequencing graph. (b) Compatibility graph. (c) Root of a hierarchical sequencing graph with branching vertex. (d) Vertex-weighted sequencing graph. (e) Compatibility graph.

The hierarchical construction of the compatibility graph preserves two properties. The vertices that are serialized with respect to each other (joined by a path in the sequencing graph) are all compatible. Those representing the concurrency factors at lower levels of the hierarchy are not compatible. Hence, the overall compatibility graph is a comparability graph, and the the clique-cover number can be computed efficiently.

This method can be extended to sequencing graphs with multiple operation types, by considering one type at a time, and assigning zero-weights to the vertices with other types. We refer the reader to reference 5 of Chapter 6 of the textbook for details.

6.6

Formulate the concurrent scheduling and binding problems in the case of multiple resource-types, by extending inequalities 6.7, 6.8, 6.9 and 6.10. Apply the formulation to the sequencing graph of Figure 4.2, while assuming that multipliers have two-unit delay and adders one unit delay. Determine a minimum latency solution with two resources per type.

Solution

To formulate the concurrent scheduling and binding problems to handle multiple resource-types, we define new binary variables, b_{irs}, to be 1 when operation v_i is bound to instance s of resource type r, i.e. when $\beta(v_i) = (r.s)$. Then we can rewrite the set of constraints in terms of B and X as follows:

$$\sum_l x_{il} \ = \ 1 \qquad i = 0, 1, \dots, n \tag{6.1}$$

$$\sum_l l \cdot x_{il} - \sum_l l \cdot x_{jl} - d_j \ \geq \ 0 \qquad i, j = 0, 1, \dots, n : (v_j, v_i) \in E \tag{6.2}$$

$$\sum_{s=1}^{a_r} b_{irs} \ = \ 1 \qquad i = 1, 2, \dots, n_{ops} \quad r = 1, 2, \dots, n_{res} \tag{6.3}$$

$$\sum_{i:T(v_i)=r} \sum_{s=1}^{a_r} b_{irs} \sum_{m=l-d_i+1}^{l} x_{im} \ \leq \ a_r \qquad l = 1, 2, \dots, \overline{\lambda} + 1 \quad r = 1, 2, \dots, n_{res} \tag{6.4}$$

$$x_{il} \ \in \ \{0, 1\} \quad i = 0, 1, \dots, n. \quad l = 1, 2, \dots, \overline{\lambda} + 1 \tag{6.5}$$

$$b_{irs} \ \in \ \{0, 1\} \quad i = 1, 2, \dots, n_{ops}, \quad r = 1, 2, \dots, n_{res} \quad s = 1, 2, \dots a_r \tag{6.6}$$

Constraint 6.1 states that each operation has to be started once, constraint 6.2 states that the sequencing constraints must be satisfied, constraint 6.3 states that each operation has to be bound to one and only one resource of that type and constraint 6.4 states that no more than a_r operations of type r can execute concurrently.

Let us consider now the example of Figure 4.2 of the textbook. We first estimate the latency to derive an upper bound $\overline{\lambda}$. This can be found using a list scheduling algorithm. Assume this algorithm returns $\overline{\lambda} = 7$. Then, we use the ASAP and ALAP schedules (of the corresponding unconstrained problem) to derive bounds on the values of the start times. The ASAP and ALAP schedules are shown in Figures 6.10 and 6.11 respectively.

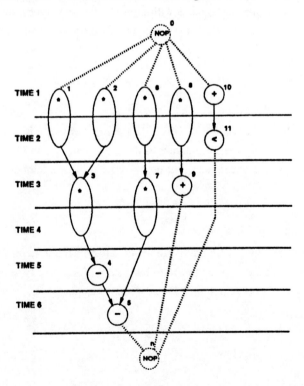

Figure 6.10: ASAP schedule

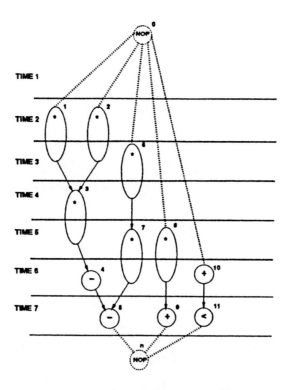

Figure 6.11: ALAP schedule with $\overline{\lambda} = 7$

Let us consider the ILP constraint one at a time. First, all operations must start only once. (Inequality 6.1).

$$x_{0,1} = 1$$
$$x_{1,1} + x_{1,2} = 1$$
$$x_{2,1} + x_{2,2} = 1$$
$$x_{3,3} + x_{3,4} = 1$$
$$x_{4,5} + x_{4,6} = 1$$
$$x_{5,6} + x_{5,7} = 1$$
$$x_{6,1} + x_{6,2} + x_{6,3} = 1$$
$$x_{7,3} + x_{7,4} + x_{7,5} = 1$$
$$x_{8,1} + x_{8,2} + x_{8,3} + x_{8,4} + x_{8,5} = 1$$
$$x_{9,3} + x_{9,4} + x_{9,5} + x_{9,6} + x_{9,7} = 1$$
$$x_{10,1} + x_{10,2} + x_{10,3} + x_{10,4} + x_{10,5} + x_{10,6} = 1$$
$$x_{11,2} + x_{11,3} + x_{11,4} + x_{11,5} + x_{11,6} + x_{11,7} = 1$$
$$x_{n,6} + x_{n,7} = 1$$

We consider next the constraints based on sequencing (we do not report those related to the source and sink). (Inequality 6.2).

$$3x_{3,3} + 4x_{3,4} - x_{1,1} - 2x_{1,2} - 2 \geq 0$$
$$3x_{3,3} + 4x_{3,4} - x_{2,1} - 2x_{2,2} - 2 \geq 0$$
$$5x_{4,5} + 6x_{4,6} - 3x_{3,3} - 4x_{3,4} - 2 \geq 0$$
$$6x_{5,6} + 7x_{5,7} - 5x_{4,5} - 6x_{4,6} - 1 \geq 0$$
$$3x_{7,3} + 4x_{7,4} + 5x_{7,5} - x_{6,1} - 2x_{6,2} - 3x_{6,3} - 2 \geq 0$$
$$6x_{5,6} + 7x_{5,7} - 3x_{7,3} - 4x_{7,4} - 5x_{7,5} - 2 \geq 0$$
$$3x_{9,3} + 4x_{9,4} + 5x_{9,5} + 6x_{9,6} + 7x_{9,7} - x_{8,1} - 2x_{8,2} - 3x_{8,3} - 4x_{8,4} - 5x_{8,5} - 2 \geq 0$$
$$2x_{11,2} + 3x_{11,3} + 4x_{11,4} + 5x_{11,5} + 6x_{11,6} + 7x_{11,7} - x_{10,1} - 2x_{10,2} - 3x_{10,3} - 4x_{10,4} - 5x_{10,5} - 6x_{10,5} - 1 \geq 0$$

Now we consider the constraints related to B due to Inequality 6.3.

$$b_{1,1,1} + b_{1,1,2} = 1$$
$$b_{2,1,1} + b_{2,1,2} = 1$$
$$b_{3,1,1} + b_{3,1,2} = 1$$
$$b_{4,2,1} + b_{4,2,2} = 1$$
$$b_{5,2,1} + b_{5,2,2} = 1$$
$$b_{6,1,1} + b_{6,1,2} = 1$$
$$b_{7,1,1} + b_{7,1,2} = 1$$
$$b_{8,1,1} + b_{8,1,2} = 1$$
$$b_{9,2,1} + b_{9,2,2} = 1$$
$$b_{10,2,1} + b_{10,2,2} = 1$$
$$b_{11,2,1} + b_{11,2,2} = 1$$

Finally, we consider the constraints related to B due to Inequality 6.4. Note that they can be classified into two groups, one per type. Note also that the middle subscript of b is the type designator, and that is constant within each group.

$$b_{1,1,1}x_{1,1} + b_{1,1,2}x_{1,1} + b_{2,1,1}x_{2,1} + b_{2,1,2}x_{2,1} + b_{6,1,1}x_{6,1} + b_{6,1,2}x_{6,1} + b_{7,1,1}x_{7,1} + b_{7,1,2}x_{7,1} + b_{8,1,1}x_{8,1} + b_{8,1,2}x_{8,1} \leq 2$$

$$b_{1,1,1}x_{1,1} + b_{1,1,2}x_{1,1} + b_{1,1,1}x_{1,2} + b_{1,1,2}x_{1,2} + b_{2,1,1}x_{2,1} + b_{2,1,2}x_{2,1} + b_{2,1,1}x_{2,2} + b_{2,1,2}x_{2,2} +$$
$$b_{6,1,1}x_{6,1} + b_{6,1,2}x_{6,1} + b_{6,1,1}x_{6,2} + b_{6,1,2}x_{6,2} + b_{7,1,1}x_{7,1} + b_{7,1,2}x_{7,1} + b_{7,1,1}x_{7,2} + b_{7,1,2}x_{7,2} +$$
$$b_{8,1,1}x_{8,1} + b_{8,1,2}x_{8,1} + b_{8,1,1}x_{8,2} + b_{8,1,2}x_{8,2} \leq 2$$

$$b_{1,1,1}x_{1,2} + b_{1,1,2}x_{1,2} + b_{2,1,1}x_{2,2} + b_{2,1,2}x_{2,2} + b_{3,1,1}x_{3,3} + b_{3,1,2}x_{3,3} + b_{6,1,1}x_{6,2} + b_{6,1,2}x_{6,2} + b_{6,1,1}x_{6,3} + b_{6,1,2}x_{6,3} +$$
$$b_{7,1,1}x_{7,2} + b_{7,1,2}x_{7,2} + b_{7,1,1}x_{7,3} + b_{7,1,2}x_{7,3} + b_{8,1,1}x_{8,2} + b_{8,1,2}x_{8,2} + b_{8,1,1}x_{8,3} + b_{8,1,2}x_{8,3} \leq 2$$

$$b_{3,1,1}x_{3,3} + b_{3,1,2}x_{3,3} + b_{3,1,1}x_{3,4} + b_{3,1,2}x_{3,4} + b_{6,1,1}x_{6,3} + b_{6,1,2}x_{6,3} +$$
$$b_{7,1,1}x_{7,3} + b_{7,1,2}x_{7,3} + b_{8,1,1}x_{8,3} + b_{8,1,2}x_{8,3} + b_{8,1,1}x_{8,4} + b_{8,1,2}x_{8,4} \leq 2$$

$$b_{3,1,1}x_{3,4} + b_{3,1,2}x_{3,4} + b_{8,1,1}x_{8,4} + b_{8,1,2}x_{8,4} + b_{8,1,1}x_{8,5} + b_{8,1,2}x_{8,5} \leq 2$$

$$b_{8,1,1}x_{8,5} + b_{8,1,2}x_{8,5} \leq 2$$

$$b_{10,2,1}x_{10,1} + b_{10,2,2}x_{10,1} \leq 2$$

$$b_{10,2,1}x_{10,2} + b_{10,2,2}x_{10,2} + b_{11,2,1}x_{11,2} + b_{11,2,2}x_{11,2} \leq 2$$

$$b_{9,2,1}x_{9,3} + b_{9,2,2}x_{9,3} + b_{10,2,1}x_{10,3} + b_{10,2,2}x_{10,3} + b_{11,2,1}x_{11,3} + b_{11,2,2}x_{11,3} \leq 2$$

$$b_{9,2,1}x_{9,4} + b_{9,2,2}x_{9,4} + b_{10,2,1}x_{10,4} + b_{10,2,2}x_{10,4} + b_{11,2,1}x_{11,4} + b_{11,2,2}x_{11,4} \leq 2$$

$$b_{4,2,1}x_{4,5} + b_{4,2,2}x_{4,5} + b_{9,2,1}x_{9,5} + b_{9,2,2}x_{9,5} + b_{10,2,1}x_{10,5} + b_{10,2,2}x_{10,5} + b_{11,2,1}x_{11,5} + b_{11,2,2}x_{11,5} \leq 2$$

$$b_{4,2,1}x_{4,6} + b_{4,2,2}x_{4,6} + b_{5,2,1}x_{5,6} + b_{5,2,2}x_{5,6} + b_{9,2,1}x_{9,6} + b_{9,2,2}x_{9,6} + b_{10,2,1}x_{10,6} + b_{10,2,2}x_{10,6} + b_{11,2,1}x_{11,6} + b_{11,2,2}x_{11,6} \leq 2$$

$$b_{5,2,1}x_{5,7} + b_{5,2,2}x_{5,7} + b_{9,2,1}x_{9,7} + b_{9,2,2}x_{9,7} + b_{11,2,1}x_{11,7} + b_{11,2,2}x_{11,7} \leq 2$$

The schedule shown in Figure 6.12 is a minimum latency solution and satisfies the ILP inequalities above. The minimum latency λ is found to be 7.

6.7

Formulate the concurrent scheduling, binding and module selection problems by an ILP model, by rewriting inequalities 6.7, 6.8, 6.9 and 6.8 in terms of n_{res} explicit resource-types that can implement an operation type. Assume a single operation type.

Solution

To formulate the concurrent scheduling, binding and module selection problems to handle multiple resource-types (but one operation type), we define new binary variables, b_{irs}, to be 1 when operation v_i is bound to instance s of resource type r, i.e. when $\beta(v_i) = (r, s)$. Resource type r is characterized by execution delay $delay_r$. An upper bound on the number of instances is $\bar{a}$. Then we can rewrite the set of constraints in terms of B and X as follows:

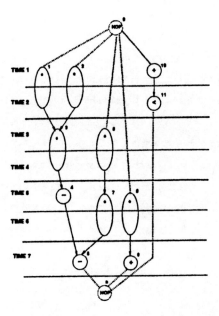

Figure 6.12: ILP solution for schedule in figure 4.2.

$$\sum_{l} x_{il} = 1 \quad i = 0, 1, \ldots, n \tag{6.7}$$

$$\sum_{l} l \cdot x_{il} - \sum_{l} l \cdot x_{jl} - d_j \geq 0 \quad i, j = 0, 1, \ldots, n : (v_j, v_i) \in E \tag{6.8}$$

$$\sum_{s=1}^{\bar{a}} b_{irs} = 1 \quad i = 1, 2, \ldots, n_{ops} \quad r = 1, 2, \ldots, n_{res} \tag{6.9}$$

$$\sum_{s=1}^{\bar{a}} b_{irs} \sum_{m=l-d_i+1}^{l} x_{im} \leq a_r \quad l = 1, 2, \ldots, \overline{\lambda} + 1 \quad i = 0, 1, \ldots, n \tag{6.10}$$

$$\sum_{s=1}^{\bar{a}} \sum_{r=1}^{n_{res}} b_{irs} delay_r - d_i = 0 \quad i = 1, 2, \ldots, n_{ops} \tag{6.11}$$

$$x_{il} \in \{0, 1\} \quad i = 0, 1, \ldots, n. \quad l = 1, 2, \ldots, \overline{\lambda} + 1 \tag{6.12}$$

$$b_{irs} \in \{0, 1\} \quad i = 1, 2, \ldots, n_{ops}. \quad r = 1, 2, \ldots, n_{res} \quad s = 1, 2, \ldots, a_r \tag{6.13}$$

6.8

Draw the compatibility and conflict graphs for the scheduled sequencing graph of Figure 5.2, assuming that it is pipelined with $\delta_0 = 2$. Determine an optimum clique partition of the former and a coloring of the latter. How many resources are required for each type?

Solution

The scheduled sequencing graph is shown in Figure 6.13.

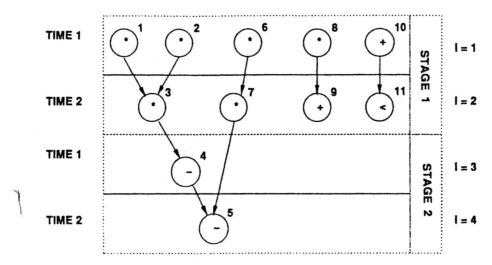

Figure 6.13: Scheduled sequencing graph with $\delta_0 = 2$.

The folded sequencing graph with binding annotation is shown in Figure 6.14.

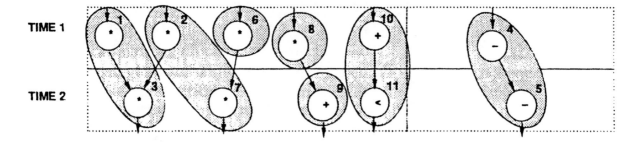

Figure 6.14: Folded sequencing graph with binding annotation.

The compatibility graph is shown in Figure 6.15, and an optimal clique partition of the compatibility graph in Figure 6.16. Four multipliers and three ALUs are needed.

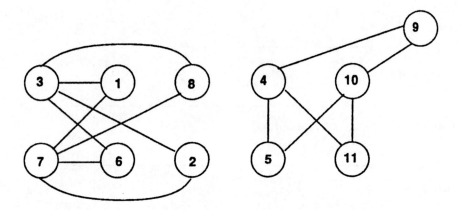

Figure 6.15: Compatibility graph for the pipelined sequencing graph.

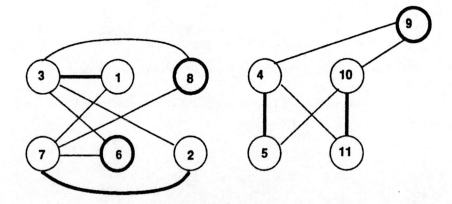

Figure 6.16: Clique partitions of the compatibility graphs of the multiply and ALU operations.

Chapter 7

Two-level combinational logic optimization

7.1

Consider a single-output bv-function f and its cover F. Show that if F is unate in a variable, so is f.

Solution

Without loss of generality, consider the cover F to be positive unate in variable x_j. Now the unate cover has an algebraic representation that is a single-output bv-function f consisting of a set of sum-of-products Boolean expressions where x_j either does not appear (*don't care* condition) or appears uncomplemented. Then changing x_j from 0 to 1 can only activate the product terms where it appears, i.e. x_j changing from 0 to 1 either does not affect f or f changes from 0 to 1 also. Therefore, f is unate in variable x_j.

7.2

Consider a mvi-function f and its cover F. Show that if F is weakly unate in a variable, so is f.

Solution

We consider covers in the positional cube notation. Specifically, consider cover F of function f. Let F be weakly unate in variable x_j, that can take values in $\{0, 1, \ldots, p-1\}$. This means that if we consider all implicants that depend on x_j, there is at least a column of zeros in the field corresponding to x_j. Assume that the column of zeros is in position k, $0 \le k \le p-1$. If we write f as a sum of the implicants in F, then we know that whenever x_j switched from value k to any other value, the value of f can only increase (i.e., go to 1 from 0 or remain constant). Thus, f is weakly unate in variable x_j.

7.3

Consider a mvi-function f that is strongly unate. Show that its complement is also a strongly unate function. Specialize this result to bv-functions. Show then, by counterexample, that the complement of a weakly unate function may not be unate.

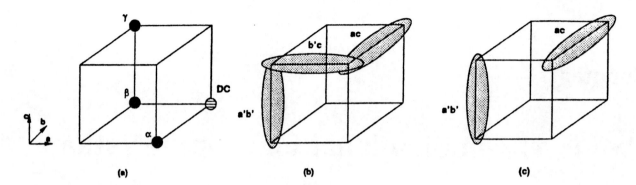

Figure 7.1: (a) Minterms of f and *don't care* set. (b) Complement computed by the sharp operator. (c) Complement computed by the sharp operator.

Solution

Without loss of generality, consider the strongly unate function f to be strongly unate in the p-valued variable x_i. Namely, assume that x_i can take values in the ordered set $(0, 1, \ldots, p-1)$.

Since $f = x^{\{0\}} f_{x\{0\}} + x^{\{1\}} f_{x\{1\}} + \ldots + x^{\{p-1\}} f_{x\{p-1\}}$, by Theorem 2.5.2 (of the textbook) we can write $f' = x^{\{0\}} f'_{x\{0\}} + x^{\{1\}} f'_{x\{1\}} + \ldots + x^{\{p-1\}} f'_{x\{p-1\}}$, by just specializing the theorem to the case in which $\odot$ is replaced by $\oplus$ and g is replaced by 1. (Thus $f \odot g = f \oplus 1 = f'$).

Recall that because of the strong unateness of f we have: $f_{x\{0\}} < f_{x\{1\}} < \ldots < f_{x\{p-1\}}$. However, since $f < g$ implies $f' > g'$, we have: $f'_{x\{0\}} > f_{x\{1\}} > \ldots > f^{x\{p-1\}}$, which shows the strong unateness of the complement.

This result specializes to binary-valued functions by choosing $p = 1$.

Now let us consider the case of a weakly unate function, in particular: $f = a^{\{1\}} x^{\{1\}} + a^{\{0\}} x^{\{2\}}$, where a is binary valued and x is ternary valued. Function f is weakly unate in x, because: $f_{x\{0\}} = 0; f_{x\{1\}} = a^{\{1\}}; f_{x\{2\}} = a^{\{0\}}$ and $f_{x\{0\}} < f_{x\{1\}}$ and $f_{x\{0\}} < f_{x\{2\}}$.

Now let us complement f. Thus: $f' = (a^{\{1\}} x^{\{1\}} + a^{\{0\}} x^{\{2\}})' = (a^{\{0\}} + x^{\{0.2\}})(a^{\{1\}} + x^{\{0.1\}}) = a^{\{0\}} x^{\{0.1\}} + a^{\{1\}} x^{\{0.2\}} + x^{\{0\}}$ Now we have $f'_{x\{0\}} = 1; f_{x\{1\}} = a^{\{0\}}; f_{x\{2\}} = a^{\{1\}}$ and thus the complement is not weakly unate.

7.4

Consider the function whose *on set* is $F^{ON} = ab'c' + a'bc' + a'bc$ and whose *dc set* is $F^{DC} = abc'$. Represent the *on set* and *dc set* in the positional cube notation and compute the *off set* by using the sharp operator. Repeat the *off set* computation by using the disjoint sharp operator.

Solution

The positional cube notation for *on set* is $F^{ON} = ab'c' + a'bc' + a'bc$ is

a	b	c
01	10	10
10	01	10
10	01	01

and for *dc set* is $F^{DC} = abc'$ we have

a	b	c
01	01	10

Now we can compute the *off set* by using the sharp operator:

$$11\ 11\ 11\ \#\ 01\ 10\ 10 = \begin{matrix} 10 & 11 & 11 \\ 11 & 01 & 11 \\ 11 & 11 & 01 \end{matrix} = F1$$

$$F1\ \#\ 10\ 01\ 10 = \begin{matrix} 10 & 10 & 11 \\ 10 & 11 & 01 \\ 01 & 01 & 11 \\ 11 & 01 & 01 \\ 01 & 11 & 01 \\ 11 & 10 & 01 \\ 11 & 11 & 01 \end{matrix} = F2 = \begin{matrix} 10 & 10 & 11 \\ 11 & 11 & 01 \\ 01 & 01 & 11 \\ 11 & 10 & 01 \end{matrix} = \begin{matrix} 10 & 10 & 11 \\ 11 & 11 & 01 \\ 01 & 01 & 11 \end{matrix}$$

$$F2\ \#\ 10\ 01\ 01 = \begin{matrix} 10 & 10 & 11 \\ 10 & 10 & 10 \\ 01 & 11 & 01 \\ 11 & 10 & 01 \\ 01 & 01 & 11 \\ 01 & 01 & 10 \end{matrix} = F3 = \begin{matrix} 10 & 10 & 11 \\ 11 & 10 & 01 \\ 01 & 11 & 01 \\ 01 & 01 & 11 \end{matrix}$$

$$F3\ \#\ 01\ 01\ 10 = \begin{matrix} 10 & 10 & 11 \\ 11 & 10 & 01 \\ 01 & 11 & 01 \end{matrix}$$

Finally, we compute the *off set* by using disjoint the sharp operator. We will simplify our task by writing the cover $F^{ON} \cup F^{DC}$ in a more compact form:

$$F^{ON} \cup F^{DC} = \begin{matrix} 01 & 10 & 10 \\ 10 & 01 & 10 \\ 10 & 01 & 01 \\ 01 & 01 & 10 \end{matrix} = \begin{matrix} 10 & 01 & 11 \\ 01 & 11 & 10 \end{matrix}$$

So the computation is as follows:

$$11\ 11\ 11\ \circledast\ 10\ 01\ 11 = \begin{matrix} 01 & 11 & 11 \\ 10 & 10 & 11 \end{matrix}$$

$$F1\ \circledast\ 01\ 11\ 10 = \begin{matrix} 01 & 11 & 01 \\ 10 & 10 & 11 \end{matrix}$$

Note that the disjoint sharp complementation results in one less implicant than the sharp complementation by excluding a non-disjoint implicant which is already covered by the other two. The cover of the complement computed by the sharp and disjoint sharp operators are shown in Figure 7.1.

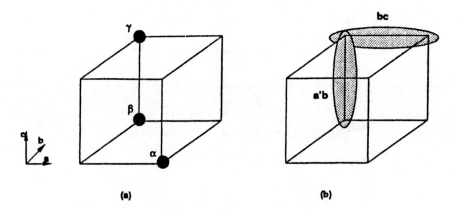

Figure 7.2: (a) Minterms of f. (b) Cubes bc and $a'b$.

7.5

Consider the function $f = ab'c' + a'bc' + a'bc$. Determine whether f contains cube bc by checking the tautology of the cofactor. Use covers in the positional cube notation and show all steps. Repeat the containment check for cube $a'b$.

Solution

The positional cube notation for f is as follows:

	a	b	c
α	01	10	10
β	10	01	10
γ	10	01	01

Also $C(bc) = 11\ 01\ 01$ and $C(a'b) = 10\ 01\ 11$. Function f is shown in Figure 7.2 (a) and cubes bc and $a'b$ in Figure 7.2 (b) respectively.

Now let us determine whether f contains cube bc by checking the tautology of the cofactor. We compute f_{bc} by computing the cofactor of each row:

$\alpha_{bc} = \emptyset$ because α and bc have a void intersection.

$\beta_{bc} = \emptyset$ because β and bc have a void intersection.

$\gamma_{bc} = 10\ 11\ 11$.

Since γ_{bc} is the only non-empty cofactor and it is not the universal cube, f_{bc} is not a tautology and so bc is not contained by f.

Next let us determine whether f contains cube $a'b$. We compute $f_{a'b}$:

$\alpha_{a'b} = \emptyset$ because α and $a'b$ have a void intersection.

$\beta_{a'b} = 11\ 11\ 10$.

$\gamma_{a'b} = 11\ 11\ 01$.

Cofactor f_{bc} is a tautology, and $a'b$ is contained by f.

7.6

Show that $f' = x \cdot f'_x + x' \cdot f'_{x'}$.

Solution

$f = x \cdot f_x + x' \cdot f_{x'}$ by the expansion theorem.

$\Rightarrow f' = (x \cdot f_x + x' \cdot f_{x'})'$

$\Rightarrow f' = (x \cdot f_x)' \cdot (x' \cdot f_{x'})'$ by De Morgan's law.

$\Rightarrow f' = (x' + f'_x) \cdot (x + f'_{x'})$ by De Morgan's law.

$\Rightarrow f' = x' \cdot x + x \cdot f'_x + f'_{x'} \cdot f'_x + x' \cdot f'_{x'}$

Since $x' \cdot x = 0$ and $x \cdot f'_x + x' \cdot f'_{x'} \supset f'_{x'} \cdot f'_x$, it follows that:

$$f' = x \cdot f'_x + x' \cdot f'_{x'}$$

7.7

Show that all primes of a unate function are essential.

Solution

The proof follows Reference 4 of the textbook (with a notation consistent with the textbook). First we need to prove the following lemma:

Lemma *Let C be a unate cover, S a subset of the cubes of C, and c any cube of C. Then $c \subseteq S$ if and only if $c \subseteq s$, for some $s \in S$.*

Proof. Without loss of generality we assume that the function whose cover is C has only binary variables and has a single output. This can be extended to multi-valued variables (by assuming a strong unate cover) and to multi-output functions (by considering a single output function where the multi-output field is a mv-variable of the new single-output function). Also, assume the function is positive unate.

We prove the sufficient condition first. If $c \subseteq s$, then $c \subseteq S$ trivially, because $s \in S$.

We prove the necessary condition next. Every cube in C covers cube 01 01 ... 01, because for every literal c_i of every cube of C, we have either $c_i = 11$ or $c_i = 01$. Since S is a subset of C, then every $s \in S$ includes also the cube 01 01 ... 01, and $c \cap s \neq \emptyset$.

Suppose now that $c \subseteq S$. Then S_c is a tautology. Since $S \subseteq C$, and C is a unate cover, then S is also a unate cover. By Theorem 7.3.2 (of the textbook) S_c is a tautology implies that $U \in S_c$ (S_c contains the universal cube U, i.e. there is a row of all 1s.) Thus, there is a cube $s \subseteq S$ which includes c. Namely the cube of $s \in S$ such that $s_c = U$ (i.e. the cube which generated the row of all 1s). $\square$

Now we can prove what we were asked:

Theorem *Every prime of a unate function f is essential.*

Proof. Let P be the set of all primes of F, the unate cover of the unate function f. Suppose there exists $p \in P$ which is not essential. Then there exists $S \subseteq P$ and p not $\in S$ such that $p \subseteq S$. By the lemma above, there is $s \in S$ such that $p \subseteq s$. This contradicts the hypothesis that p is prime. Thus, all primes of a unate function are essential.

7.8

Design a recursive algorithm to check if an expanded implicant is covered by $F^{ON} \cup F^{DC}$.

Solution

Let $G = F^{ON} \cup F^{DC}$ and α the (expanded) implicant to be checked for inclusion in G. Covering can be checked by verifying whether G_α is a tautology, which can be done by the recursive algorithm shown in the textbook. We describe next a direct covering check algorithm, as used by program Presto.

$CHECK\_CONTAINMENT(G, \alpha)$ {
    if (a cube of G covers α) **return** (TRUE);
    if (no cube of G intersects α) **return** (FALSE);
    select *don't care* variable i in α;
    return ($CHECK\_CONTAINMENT(G, \alpha_{|i=0}) \cdot CHECK\_CONTAINMENT(G, \alpha_{|i=1})$);
    }

The first two conditional tests can be trivially done by bit-wise comparisons, and a *don't care* variable must exist in α if the first two tests evaluate FALSE . The algorithm just expands the *don't care* entry and recurs. In the worst case, all minterms of α are generated. Heuristics guide the selection of the splitting variable to terminate the search earlier.

7.9

Consider a mvi-function f and its cover F. Show that for any p-valued variable x:

$$supercube(F') = supercube(\cup_{k=0}^{p-1} C(x^{\{k\}}) \cap supercube(F'_{x^{\{k\}}})).$$

Solution

It is worth while remembering that the $supercube(C)$ is a single cube; $supercube(C) \supseteq C$ and $supercube(supercube(C)) = supercube(C)$.

We first prove the following:

$$supercube(F) = supercube(\cup_{k=0}^{p-1} C(x^{\{k\}}) \cap supercube(F_{x^{\{k\}}}))$$

First of all:

$$supercube(C(x^{\{k\}}) \cap supercube(F_{x^{\{k\}}})) = C(x^{\{k\}}) \cap supercube(F_{x^{\{k\}}})$$

because $C(x^{\{k\}})$ is a single cube. Since:

$$supercube(F) \supseteq supercube(C(x^{\{k\}}) \cap F_{x^{\{k\}}})$$

then:

$$supercube(F) \supseteq C(x^{\{k\}}) \cap supercube(F_{x^{\{k\}}})$$

and considering all the possible values of $x^{\{k\}}$, we have:

$$supercube(F) \supseteq \cup_{k=0}^{p-1} \; C(x^{\{k\}}) \cap supercube(F_{x^{\{k\}}})$$

Now apply the $supercube()$ operator to both sides:

$$supercube(supercube(F)) \supseteq supercube(\cup_{k=0}^{p-1} \; C(x^{\{k\}}) \cap supercube(F_{x^{\{k\}}}))$$

or equivalently:

$$supercube(F) \supseteq supercube(\cup_{k=0}^{p-1} \; C(x^{\{k\}}) \cap supercube(F_{x^{\{k\}}})) \qquad '$$

Since:

$$F = \cup_{k=0}^{p-1} \; C(x^{\{k\}}) \cap F_{x^{\{k\}}} \subseteq \cup_{k=0}^{p-1} \; C(x^{\{k\}}) \cap supercube(F_{x^{\{k\}}})$$

then:

$$supercube(F) \subseteq supercube(\cup_{k=0}^{p-1} \; C(x^{\{k\}}) \cap supercube(F_{x^{\{k\}}}))$$

This result together with what we showed previously yields:

$$supercube(F) = supercube(\cup_{k=0}^{p-1} \; C(x^{\{k\}}) \cap supercube(F_{x^{\{k\}}}))$$

We also know that:

$$F' = \cup_{k=0}^{p-1} \; C(x^{\{k\}}) \cap F'_{x^{\{k\}}}$$

By applying the property shown above, we get the desired result:

$$supercube(F') = supercube(\cup_{k=0}^{p-1} \; C(x^{\{k\}}) \cap supercube(F'_{x^{\{k\}}}))$$

7.10

Consider function $f = a'd' + a'b + ab' + ac'd$. Form a cover in the positional cube notation and compute all primes and all essential primes, using the methods outlined in Sections 7.3.4 and 7.4.4 respectively. Show all steps. Compare your results with Figure 7.5 (a).

Solution

The positional cube notation for f is as follows:

a	b	c	d
10	11	11	10
10	01	11	11
01	10	11	11
01	11	10	01

First we find the primes of f using the method outlined in Section 7.3.4:

We begin by splitting around $a = 01\ 11\ 11$:

$$f_a = \begin{array}{cccc} 11 & 10 & 11 & 11 \\ 11 & 11 & 10 & 01 \end{array} \quad f_{a'} = \begin{array}{cccc} 11 & 11 & 11 & 10 \\ 11 & 01 & 11 & 11 \end{array}$$

Both of the resulting covers are unate and minimal with respect to single implicant containment. Thus

$$P(f_a) = \begin{array}{cccc} 11 & 10 & 11 & 11 \\ 11 & 11 & 10 & 01 \end{array} \quad P(f_{a'}) = \begin{array}{cccc} 11 & 11 & 11 & 10 \\ 11 & 01 & 11 & 11 \end{array}$$

Next we have

$$P_1 = C(a) \cap P(f_a) = \begin{array}{c|cccc} \alpha_1 & 01 & 10 & 11 & 11 \\ \alpha_2 & 01 & 11 & 10 & 01 \end{array} \quad P_2 = C(a') \cap P(f_{a'}) = \begin{array}{c|cccc} \beta_1 & 10 & 11 & 11 & 10 \\ \beta_2 & 10 & 01 & 11 & 11 \end{array}$$

Now $P_3 = CONSENSUS(P_1, P_2)$.

$$CONSENSUS(\alpha_1, \beta_1) = 11 \quad 10 \quad 11 \quad 10 \qquad CONSENSUS(\alpha_1, \beta_2) = \emptyset$$

$$CONSENSUS(\alpha_2, \beta_1) = \emptyset \qquad CONSENSUS(\alpha_2, \beta_2) = 11 \quad 01 \quad 10 \quad 01$$

Therefore:

$$SCC(P_1 \cup P_2 \cup P_3) = \begin{array}{cccc} 01 & 10 & 11 & 11 \\ 01 & 11 & 10 & 01 \\ 10 & 11 & 11 & 10 \\ 10 & 01 & 11 & 11 \\ 11 & 10 & 11 & 10 \\ 11 & 01 & 10 & 01 \end{array}$$

And so the primes found are ab', $ac'd$, $a'd'$, $a'b$, $b'd'$, and $bc'd$, as shown in Figure 7.5 (a) of the textbook.

Next we find the essential primes for f using the method outlined in Section 7.4.4. Therefore we apply the following formula to test each prime:

$$H = CONSENSUS(((F^{ON} \cup F^{DC})\#p), p)$$

where p is a generic prime. For our problem $F^{DC} = \emptyset$.

First consider $p = 10\ 11\ 11\ 10$. ($p = \alpha$ in Figure 7.5 a.) Then:

$$f_1 = F_{ON}\ \#\ 10\ 11\ 11\ 10 = \begin{array}{cccc} 01 & 10 & 11 & 11 \\ 01 & 11 & 10 & 01 \\ 10 & 01 & 11 & 01 \end{array}$$

Now we can calculate H for f_1:

$$H = CONSENSUS(f_1, 10\ 11\ 11\ 10) = \begin{array}{cccc} 11 & 10 & 11 & 10 \\ 10 & 01 & 11 & 11 \end{array}$$

Then:

$$H_{a'd'} = \begin{array}{cccc} 11 & 01 & 11 & 11 \\ 11 & 10 & 11 & 11 \end{array}$$

which is a tautology, and so $a'd'$ is not essential.

Second, consider $p = 10\ 01\ 11\ 11$. ($p = \gamma$ in Figure 7.5 a.) Then:

$$
f_2 = F_{ON}\ \#\ 10\ 01\ 11\ 11 = \begin{array}{cccc} 01 & 10 & 11 & 11 \\ 01 & 11 & 10 & 01 \\ 11 & 10 & 11 & 10 \end{array}
$$

We can calculate the H for f_2:

$$
H = \mathcal{CONSENSUS}(f_2, 10\ 01\ 11\ 11) = \begin{array}{cccc} 11 & 01 & 10 & 01 \\ 10 & 11 & 11 & 10 \end{array}
$$

Now:

$$
H_{a'b} = \begin{array}{cccc} 11 & 11 & 10 & 01 \\ 11 & 11 & 11 & 10 \end{array}
$$

which is not a tautology, and so $a'b$ is essential.

Third consider $p = 01\ 10\ 11\ 11$. ($p = \delta$ in Figure 7.5 a.) Then:

$$
f_3 = F_{ON}\ \#\ 01\ 10\ 11\ 11 = \begin{array}{cccc} 10 & 01 & 11 & 11 \\ 10 & 11 & 11 & 10 \\ 11 & 01 & 10 & 01 \end{array}
$$

Now we can calculate H for f_3:

$$
H = \mathcal{CONSENSUS}(f_3, 01\ 10\ 11\ 11) = \begin{array}{cccc} 11 & 10 & 11 & 10 \\ 01 & 11 & 10 & 01 \end{array}
$$

Then:

$$
H_{ab'} = \begin{array}{cccc} 11 & 11 & 11 & 10 \\ 11 & 11 & 10 & 01 \end{array}
$$

which is not a tautology, and so ab' is essential.

Fourth, consider $p = 01\ 11\ 10\ 01$. ($p = \varepsilon$ in Figure 7.5 a.) Then:

$$
f_4 = F_{ON}\ \#\ 01\ 11\ 10\ 01 = \begin{array}{cccc} 11 & 10 & 11 & 10 \\ 10 & 01 & 11 & 11 \\ 01 & 10 & 01 & 11 \end{array}
$$

We can calculate the H for f_4:

$$
H = \mathcal{CONSENSUS}(f_4, 01\ 11\ 10\ 01) = \begin{array}{cccc} 01 & 10 & 10 & 11 \\ 11 & 01 & 10 & 01 \\ 01 & 10 & 11 & 01 \end{array}
$$

Now:

$$
H_{ac'd} = \begin{array}{cccc} 11 & 10 & 11 & 11 \\ 11 & 01 & 11 & 11 \\ 11 & 10 & 11 & 11 \end{array}
$$

which is a tautology, and so $ac'd$ is not essential.

Fifth, consider $p = 11\ 10\ 11\ 10$. ($p = \beta$ in Figure 7.5 a.) Then:

$$f_5 = F_{ON} \# 11\ 10\ 11\ 10 = \begin{matrix} 10 & 01 & 11 & 11 \\ 01 & 11 & 10 & 01 \\ 01 & 10 & 11 & 01 \end{matrix}$$

Now we can calculate H for f_5:

$$H = CONSENSUS(f_5, 11\ 10\ 11\ 10) = \begin{matrix} 10 & 11 & 11 & 10 \\ 01 & 10 & 10 & 11 \\ 01 & 10 & 11 & 11 \end{matrix}$$

Then:

$$H_{b'd'} = \begin{matrix} 10 & 11 & 11 & 11 \\ 01 & 11 & 10 & 11 \\ 01 & 11 & 11 & 11 \end{matrix}$$

which is a tautology, and so $b'd'$ is not essential.

Finally, consider $p = 11\ 01\ 10\ 01$. ($p = \zeta$ in Figure 7.5 a.) Then:

$$f_6 = F_{ON} \# 11\ 01\ 10\ 01 = \begin{matrix} 01 & 10 & 11 & 11 \\ 10 & 11 & 11 & 10 \\ 10 & 01 & 01 & 11 \end{matrix}$$

We can calculate the H for f_6:

$$H = CONSENSUS(f_6, 11\ 01\ 10\ 01) = \begin{matrix} 01 & 11 & 10 & 01 \\ 10 & 01 & 10 & 11 \\ 10 & 01 & 11 & 01 \end{matrix}$$

Now:

$$H_{ac'd} = \begin{matrix} 01 & 11 & 11 & 11 \\ 10 & 11 & 11 & 11 \\ 10 & 11 & 11 & 11 \end{matrix}$$

which is a tautology, and so $ac'd$ is not essential.

The results agree with Figure 7.5; all six prime implicants in the figure were found and $\gamma = a'b$ and $\delta = ab'$ are the only two essential primes found.

7.11

Show how mvi-minimization can be done using a bv-minimizer by specifying an appropriate *don't care* set.

Solution

Mvi-variables can be represented by 1-hot encoding. Thus, a p-valued variable can be represented by p binary-valued variables. When considering the field associated with the p bv-variables (representing a p-valued variable), the cube representing no variables and those cubes representing two (or more) variables are *don't care* conditions.

For example, consider a 4-valued variable. To use a bv-minimizer, we could use one-hot encoding for the four values: {1000; 0100; 0010; 0001 }. Condition 0000 is a *don't care* . So are all cubes with two (or more) 1s. It suffices to list all cubes with two 1s, the other entries being *don't cares* .

Using symbols in the set $\{0, 1, *\}$, the *don't care* set is:

$$
\begin{array}{cccc}
0 & 0 & 0 & 0 \\
1 & 1 & * & * \\
1 & * & 1 & * \\
1 & * & * & 1 \\
* & 1 & 1 & * \\
* & 1 & * & 1 \\
* & * & 1 & 1 \\
\end{array}
$$

Equivalently, in the positional cube notation, the four care values are:

$$
\begin{array}{cccc}
01 & 11 & 11 & 11 \\
11 & 01 & 11 & 11 \\
11 & 11 & 01 & 11 \\
11 & 11 & 11 & 01 \\
\end{array}
$$

and the *don't care* set is:

$$
\begin{array}{cccc}
10 & 10 & 10 & 10 \\
01 & 01 & 11 & 11 \\
01 & 11 & 01 & 11 \\
01 & 11 & 11 & 01 \\
11 & 01 & 01 & 11 \\
11 & 01 & 11 & 01 \\
11 & 11 & 01 & 01 \\
\end{array}
$$

7.12

The Natchez Indian culture has four classes: *Suns, Nobles, Honored* and *Stinkards*. Within this culture, the allowed marriages and the resulting offspring is given by the following table:

Mother	Father	Offspring
Sun	Stinkard	Sun
Noble	Stinkard	Noble
Honored	Stinkard	Honored
Stinkard	Sun	Noble
Stinkard	Noble	Honored
Stinkard	Honored	Stinkard
Stinkard	Stinkard	Stinkard

The remaining marriages are not allowed. Represent the condition that yields a Stinkard offspring by a single symbolic implicant. Then form a minimal symbolic representation of the disallowed marriages. Label the offspring field as 'none' in this case.

Solution

The condition that yields a Stinkard offspring is represented by the following symbolic implicant:

$$\text{Stinkard} \quad \text{(Honored, Stinkard)} \quad \text{Stinkard}$$

Note that the second symbolic literal is compound.

Now consider the disallowed marriages:

- A Sun woman is not allowed to marry a Sun, Noble, or Honored man:

$$\text{Sun} \quad \text{(Sun,Noble,Honored)} \quad \text{None}$$

- A Noble woman is not allowed to marry a Sun, Noble, or Honored man:

$$\text{Noble} \quad \text{(Sun,Noble,Honored)} \quad \text{None}$$

- A Honored woman is not allowed to marry a Sun, Noble, or Honored man:

$$\text{Honored} \quad \text{(Sun,Noble,Honored)} \quad \text{None}$$

Overall, the disallowed marriages can be represented by:

$$\text{(Sun,Noble,Honored)} \quad \text{(Sun,Noble,Honored)} \quad \text{None}$$

7.13

Consider an input encoding problem characterized by constraint matrix $\mathbf{A}$. Show that a valid encoding matrix $\mathbf{E}$ remains valid for any permutation or complementation of its columns.

Solution

Recall that the input encoding problem for n_s symbols is modeled by a binary constraint matrix $\mathbf{A} \in B^{n_r \times n_s}$, with n_r rows representing constraints and by an encoding binary matrix $\mathbf{E} \in B^{n_s \times n_b}$, whose rows are the codes of the symbols with n_b bits. An encoding matrix $\mathbf{E}$ is valid if (i) for each row of $\mathbf{A}$ the supercube of the rows of $\mathbf{E}$ corresponding to the 1's in that row does not intersect any of the rows of $\mathbf{E}$ corresponding to the 0's in that row, and (ii) all the rows are distinct.

Condition (ii) is obviously preserved under permutation and complementation, because the Hamming distance between to codes does not change.

Condition (i) can be checked while considering one row of $\mathbf{A}$ at a time. Consider a generic row $\mathbf{a}^T$: it induces a bi-partition of the symbol set into S_1 and S_0, and equivalently a partition of the rows of $\mathbf{E}$ into two blocks. Condition (i) is satisfied if and only if the supercube of the rows of $\mathbf{E}$ corresponding to S_1 does not intersect any row of $\mathbf{E}$ corresponding to S_0, i.e. if the Hamming distance is larger than zero. Let the supercube be denoted by $\mathbf{c}$.

Any column permutation of $\mathbf{E}$ induces a permutation of the corresponding entries of $\mathbf{c}$ and therefore it does not affect Hamming distance between $\mathbf{c}$ and any row of $\mathbf{E}$.

Consider next a column complementation. If the corresponding entry in **c** is a *don't care* condition, this entry is not affected by the complementation. On the other hand, the contribution to the Hamming distance of this entry is zero, and it is preserved by the complementation. Alternatively, if the entry in **c** is a 1 (or 0), the entry will be complemented. But since all entries of that column of **E** are complemented, the contribution to the Hamming distance will not change. Since this is true for any column complementation, the Hamming distance is preserved. As a result, column permutation and complementation of **E** do not affect its validity.

7.14

Consider the input encoding problem specified by matrix:

$$\mathbf{A} = \begin{bmatrix} 1 & 1 & 0 & 0 \\ 0 & 1 & 1 & 0 \\ 0 & 0 & 1 & 1 \\ 1 & 0 & 0 & 1 \end{bmatrix}$$

where each column from left to right is associated with an element in the set:(a, b, c, d). Find a minimum-length encoding **E** satisfying the constraint. Find a minimum-length encoding **E** satisfying the constraint and such that the code of b covers the code of c. Repeat the exercise for the input encoding problem specified by matrix:

$$\mathbf{A} = \begin{bmatrix} 1 & 1 & 0 & 1 & 0 & 1 & 0 & 0 \\ 0 & 1 & 0 & 1 & 0 & 0 & 0 & 0 \\ 1 & 0 & 0 & 0 & 0 & 1 & 0 & 0 \\ 0 & 0 & 0 & 1 & 0 & 1 & 1 & 1 \\ 0 & 0 & 0 & 0 & 0 & 1 & 0 & 1 \\ 0 & 1 & 1 & 0 & 0 & 0 & 0 & 0 \\ 1 & 0 & 0 & 0 & 1 & 0 & 0 & 0 \end{bmatrix}$$

where each column from left to right is associated with an element in the set:(a, b, c, d, e, f, g, h). Use your favorite method.

Solution

We use a heuristic construction of **E** column by column, as described in the textbook.
First choose row 1 of **A** (i.e., 1 1 0 0) as first column of **E**.

$$\mathbf{E} = \begin{bmatrix} 1 \\ 1 \\ 0 \\ 0 \end{bmatrix}$$

Or, equivalently

$$CODE(a) = 1$$
$$CODE(b) = 1$$
$$CODE(c) = 0$$
$$CODE(d) = 0$$

Now, the first constraint is satisfied and can be dropped from further consideration. The third constraint is also satisfied because $[CODE(a) \cup CODE(b)] \cap [CODE(c) \cup CODE(d)] = \emptyset$ and therefore can be dropped as well.

So now we have reduced $\mathbf{A}$ to the following:

$$\mathbf{A}_{reduced} = \begin{bmatrix} 0 & 1 & 1 & 0 \\ 1 & 0 & 0 & 1 \end{bmatrix}$$

We choose second row of $\mathbf{A}_{reduced}$ as second column of $\mathbf{E}$. Thus:

$$\mathbf{E} = \begin{bmatrix} 1 & 0 \\ 1 & 1 \\ 0 & 1 \\ 0 & 0 \end{bmatrix}$$

or, equivalently:

$$\begin{aligned} CODE(a) &= 1 \quad 0 \\ CODE(b) &= 1 \quad 1 \\ CODE(c) &= 0 \quad 1 \\ CODE(d) &= 0 \quad 0 \end{aligned}$$

We need to verify that $\mathbf{E}$ satisfies indeed the covering constraint. Namely: $CODE(b) \geq CODE(c)$. This is true.

Now consider the second matrix. We use again a heuristic approach. We attempt to use a minimum number of bits. To achieve a 3-bit encoding, we need to divide by two the number of indistinguishable codes with every column. At the beginning we have 8 indistinguishable codes, which implies that we need to choose a column with four 1's (and four 0's).

We choose the first row of $\mathbf{A}$ as first column of $\mathbf{E}$:

$$\begin{aligned} CODE(a) &= 1 \\ CODE(b) &= 1 \\ CODE(c) &= 0 \\ CODE(d) &= 1 \\ CODE(e) &= 0 \\ CODE(f) &= 1 \\ CODE(g) &= 0 \\ CODE(h) &= 0 \end{aligned}$$

Now we need to choose a column that partitions $\{a, b, d, f\}$ and $\{c, e, g, h\}$ into four blocks of cardinality two each. The fourth row of $\mathbf{A}$ does the job:

$$\begin{aligned} CODE(a) &= 1 \quad 0 \\ CODE(b) &= 1 \quad 0 \\ CODE(c) &= 0 \quad 0 \\ CODE(d) &= 1 \quad 1 \\ CODE(e) &= 0 \quad 0 \\ CODE(f) &= 1 \quad 1 \\ CODE(g) &= 0 \quad 1 \\ CODE(h) &= 0 \quad 1 \end{aligned}$$

Now we need to choose a column such that:

- Partitions $\{a, b\}$, $\{c, e\}$, $\{d, f\}$ and $\{g, h\}$ into 8 blocks of 1 element each.

- Satisfies constraints related to rows 2, 3, 5, 6, and 7 of **A**.

The strategy we use is to try to assign the same code bit to symbols in the same group. For example, while trying to satisfy the constraint of the second row of **A**, we choose a 1 as third bit for b and d. Using the same idea for the other constraints we get:

$$
\begin{aligned}
CODE(a) &= 1 \quad 0 \quad 0 \\
CODE(b) &= 1 \quad 0 \quad 1 \\
CODE(c) &= 0 \quad 0 \quad 1 \\
CODE(d) &= 1 \quad 1 \quad 1 \\
CODE(e) &= 0 \quad 0 \quad 0 \\
CODE(f) &= 1 \quad 1 \quad 0 \\
CODE(g) &= 0 \quad 1 \quad 1 \\
CODE(h) &= 0 \quad 1 \quad 0
\end{aligned}
$$

or equivalently:

$$
\mathbf{E} = \begin{bmatrix}
1 & 0 & 0 \\
1 & 0 & 1 \\
0 & 0 & 1 \\
1 & 1 & 1 \\
0 & 0 & 0 \\
1 & 1 & 0 \\
0 & 1 & 1 \\
0 & 1 & 0
\end{bmatrix}
$$

The supercubes corresponding to the seven constraints are:

$$
\begin{aligned}
c_1 &= 1 \quad * \quad * \\
c_2 &= 1 \quad * \quad 1 \\
c_3 &= 1 \quad * \quad 0 \\
c_4 &= * \quad 1 \quad * \\
c_5 &= * \quad 1 \quad 0 \\
c_6 &= * \quad 0 \quad 1 \\
c_7 &= * \quad 0 \quad 0
\end{aligned}
$$

And it is possible to verify that all constraints are satisfied.

7.15

Consider the input encoding problem specified by matrix:

$$A = \begin{bmatrix} 1 & 1 & 0 & 1 & 0 & 1 & 0 & 0 \\ 0 & 1 & 0 & 1 & 0 & 0 & 0 & 0 \\ 1 & 0 & 0 & 0 & 0 & 1 & 0 & 0 \\ 0 & 0 & 0 & 1 & 0 & 1 & 1 & 1 \\ 0 & 0 & 0 & 0 & 0 & 1 & 0 & 1 \\ 0 & 1 & 1 & 0 & 0 & 0 & 0 & 0 \\ 1 & 0 & 0 & 0 & 1 & 0 & 0 & 0 \end{bmatrix}$$

Compute all seed and prime dichotomies. Formulate a covering table and solve it exactly.

Solution

This problem is best solved by using a computer program. Let the symbols be labeled as (a, b, c, d, e, f, h). The (38) seed dichotomies are the following.

({a b d f} ; {c})
({a b d f} ; {e})
({a b d f} ; {g})
({a b d f} ; {h})
({b d} ; {a})
({b d} ; {c})
({b d} ; {f})
({b d} ; {e})
({b d} ; {g})
({b d} ; {h})
({a f} ; {b})
({a f} ; {c})
({a f} ; {d})
({a f} ; {e})
({a f} ; {g})
({a f} ; {h})
({d f g h} ; {a})
({d f g h} ; {b})
({d f g h} ; {c})
({d f g h} ; {e})
({f h} ; {a})
({f h} ; {b})
({f h} ; {c})
({f h} ; {d})
({f h} ; {e})
({f h} ; {g})

({b c} ; {a})
({b c} ; {d})
({b c} ; {e})
({b c} ; {f})
({b c} ; {g})
({b c} ; {h})
({a e} ; {b})
({a e} ; {c})
({a e} ; {d})
({a e} ; {f})
({a e} ; {g})
({a e} ; {h})

The (67) prime dichotomies are the following:

({a b d f g h} ; {c e})
({a b c} ; {d e f g h})
({b c d f g h} ; {a e})
({a b e} ; {c d f g h})
({a d e f g h} ; {b c})
({a c e} ; {b d f g h})
({b c e} ; {a d f g h})
({a b d f h} ; {c e g})
({a b d f} ; {c e g h})
({a b d e f} ; {c g h})
({a b d e f h} ; {c g})
({a b d e f g h} ; {c})
({a b c d f} ; {e g h})
({a b c d f h} ; {e g})
({a b c d f g h} ; {e})
({a b c d e f} ; {g h})
({a b c d e f h} ; {g})
({a c e f h} ; {b d g})
({b d f h} ; {a c e g})
({a c f g h} ; {b d e})
({a c f h} ; {b d e g})
({a c e f} ; {b d g h})
({a e f h} ; {b c d g})
({b c d e} ; {a f g h})
({a e f g} ; {b c d h})
({a e f g h} ; {b c d})
({b c d f h} ; {a e g})
({a e g h} ; {b c d f})

({a f h} ; {b c d e g})
({a e f} ; {b c d g h})
({b c d e h} ; {a f g})
({a e h} ; {b c d f g})
({a c e f g} ; {b d h})
({a b d e} ; {c f g h})
({a b d e g} ; {c f h})
({c e f g h} ; {a b d})
({c e f h} ; {a b d g})
({a c e g h} ; {b d f})
({a c f g} ; {b d e h})
({a c e f g h} ; {b d})
({a c e h} ; {b d f g})
({a c f} ; {b d e g h})
({a b c d} ; {e f g h})
({a b c d e} ; {f g h})
({a b c d g} ; {e f h})
({a b c d e g} ; {f h})
({b c e g} ; {a d f h})
({a d e f} ; {b c g h})
({a d e f h} ; {b c g})
({a d e f g} ; {b c h})
({a b c f} ; {d e g h})
({a b c f h} ; {d e g})
({a b c e f} ; {d g h})
({a b c e f h} ; {d g})
({b c e g h} ; {a d f})
({b c e h} ; {a d f g})
({d f g h} ; {a b c e})
({b c f h} ; {a d e g})
({a d e} ; {b c f g h})
({a b c e g} ; {d f h})
({a b c g} ; {d e f h})
({a b e g} ; {c d f h})
({a c d e g} ; {b f h})
({a c d e} ; {b f g h})
({a d e g h} ; {b c f})
({a d e h} ; {b c f g})
({a f} ; {b c d e g h})

An example of a minimum cover is given by the primes:

({a b d f} ; {c e g h})
({d f g h} ; {a b c e})
({a e f h} ; {b c d g})

corresponding to the encoding:

$$E = \begin{bmatrix} 1 & 0 & 1 \\ 1 & 0 & 0 \\ 0 & 0 & 0 \\ 1 & 1 & 0 \\ 0 & 0 & 1 \\ 1 & 1 & 1 \\ 0 & 1 & 0 \\ 0 & 1 & 1 \end{bmatrix}$$

7.16

Consider the optimization of a logic unit performing $f_1 = a + b$; $f_2 = b + c$ under the assumption that the outputs feed only an OR gate. Write the Boolean relation that specifies the equivalent output patterns of the logic unit and determine a minimum (product-term and literal) compatible function. Is the minimum function unique?

Solution

Since the outputs of the logic block under consideration feed an OR gate that yields: $f_1 + f_2 = a + b + c$, output patterns {01.10.11} are equivalent.

The logic unit can be modeled by a Boolean relation as follows:

a	b	c	Out
0	0	0	{00}
0	0	1	{01, 10, 11}
0	1	0	{01, 10, 11}
0	1	1	{01, 10, 11}
1	0	0	{01, 10, 11}
1	0	1	{01, 10, 11}
1	1	0	{01, 10, 11}
1	1	1	{01, 10, 11}

The overall network is shown in picture (a) of Figure 7.3. Examples of compatible functions and their implementations are shown in Figures 7.3 (b,c,d), and their covers are listed below.

a	b	c	Out
01	11	11	10
11	01	11	10
11	11	01	01

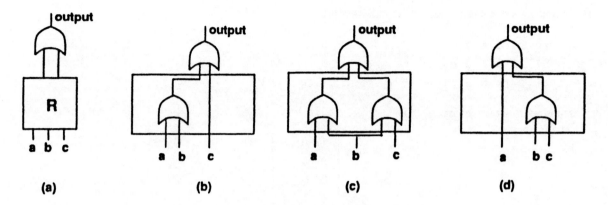

Figure 7.3: Boolean Relation and boxed equivalents

a	b	c	Out
01	11	11	10
11	01	11	11
11	11	01	01

a	b	c	Out
01	11	11	01
11	01	11	10
11	11	01	10

There are two compatible functions with a minimum number of product-terms and literals, shown in Figures
7.3 (b,d) respectively.

Chapter 8

Multiple-level combinational logic optimization

8.1

Prove that given two algebraic expressions $f_{dividend}$ and $f_{divisor}$, the algebraic quotient of the former by the latter is empty if any of the following condition applies:

- $f_{divisor}$ contains a variable not in $f_{dividend}$.

- $f_{divisor}$ contains a cube not contained in any cube of $f_{dividend}$.

- $f_{divisor}$ contains more terms than $f_{dividend}$ (i.e. $m > n$).

- The count of any variable in $f_{divisor}$ is larger than in $f_{dividend}$.

Solution

Recall that since the terms of all algebraic expressions are minimal with respect to single cube containment, there are no repeated cubes.

- Assume $f_{divisor}$ contains variable x not in $f_{dividend}$. Since $f_{dividend} = f_{divisor} \cdot f_{quotient} + f_{remainder}$ then variable x appears also in $f_{dividend}$ unless $f_{quotient}$ is empty.

- Assume $f_{divisor}$ contains cube C not in $f_{dividend}$. Since $f_{dividend} = f_{divisor} \cdot f_{quotient} + f_{remainder}$ then cube C is contained is at least a cube of $f_{dividend}$ unless $f_{quotient}$ is empty.

- Since $f_{dividend} = f_{divisor} \cdot f_{quotient} + f_{remainder}$, the number of cubes in $f_{dividend}$ is larger than, or equal to, the product of the number of cubes in $f_{divisor}$ times number of cubes in $f_{quotient}$. Thus, the number of cubes in $f_{divisor}$ cannot exceed the number of cubes in $f_{dividend}$ unless $f_{quotient}$ is empty.

- Assume $f_{divisor}$ contains variable x whose count n_x is larger than in $f_{dividend}$. Since $f_{dividend} = f_{divisor} \cdot f_{quotient} + f_{remainder}$ then variable x appears in $f_{dividend}$ at least n_x times, unless $f_{quotient}$ is empty.

8.2

Design an algorithm that finds all 0-level kernels of a function.

Solution

Recall that a 0-level kernel is a kernel which has no kernels except itself.

The following algorithm is a modification of the $KERNELS$ algorithm. As for the $KERNELS$ algorithm, it is applicable to cube-free expressions. Thus, either the function f is cube-free or it is made so by dividing it by its largest cube factor, determined by the intersection of the support sets of all its cubes. The pointer j is set initially to 1.

Note that it differs from $KERNELS$ in the conditional update of K.

```
ZERO_KERNELS(f, j){
    K = ∅;
    for i = j to n {
        if(|CUBES(f, x_i)| ≥ 2) {                    /* skip cases where f/x yields one cube */
            C = largest cube containing x such that CUBES(f, C) = CUBES(f, x);
            if (x_k ∉ C ∀k < i)                      /* skip if C contains already considered variables */
                K = K ∪ ZERO_KERNELS(f/f^C, i + 1);
        }
    }
    if (K = ∅)   K = f;                               /* add f to kernel set if it has no kernels */
    return(K);
}
```

8.3

Design an algorithm that finds just one 0-level kernel of a function.

Solution

The following algorithm is another modification of the $KERNELS$ algorithm. Considerations similar to those presented for the previous problem apply.

```
ONE_ZERO_KERNEL(f, j){
    K = ∅;
    for i = j to n {
        if(|CUBES(f, x_i)| ≥ 2) {                    /* skip cases where f/x yields one cube */
            C = largest cube containing x such that CUBES(f, C) = CUBES(f, x);
            if (x_k ∉ C ∀k < i)                      /* skip if C contains already considered variables */
                return ( ONE_ZERO_KERNEL(f/f^C, i + 1) );
        }
    }
    return(f);
}
```

8.4

Consider the logic network defined by the following expressions:

$$x = ad' + a'b' + a'd' + bc + bd' + ac$$

$$y = a + b$$

$$z = a'c' + a'd' + b'c' + b'd' + e$$

$$u = a'c + a'd + b'd + e'$$

Draw the logic network graph. Outputs are $\{x, y, z, u\}$. Perform the algebraic division f_x / f_y and show all steps. Substitute y into f_x and redraw the network graph. Compute all kernels and co-kernels of z and u. Extract a multiple-cube subexpression common to f_z and f_u. Show all steps. Redraw the network graph.

Solution

The logic network graph is shown in Figure 8.1.

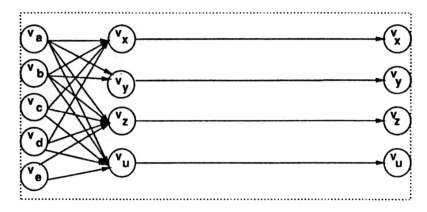

Figure 8.1: Initial logic network graph.

The algebraic division f_x / f_y is done as follows. At the first iteration ($i = 1$) we have: $C_1^y = a$; $D = \{ad', ac\}$ and $D_1 = \{d', c\}$. Thus Q is initialized to $\{d', c\}$. At the second iteration ($i = 2$) we have: $C_2^y = b$; $D = \{bd', bc\}$ and $D_2 = \{d', c\}$. Thus $Q = \{d', c\}$. Therefore $f_{quotient} = c + d'$ and $f_{remainder} = a'b' + a'd'$.

Substituting y into f_x yields $x = y(c + d') + a'b' + a'd'$. The corresponding network graph is shown in Figure 8.2.

Next we compute all kernels and co-kernels of z and u, and then extract a multiple-cube subexpression common to f_z and f_u.

Consider $z = a'c' + a'd' + b'c' + b'd' + e$. Kernels of z are: $\{a' + b', c' + d', a'c' + a'd' + b'c' + b'd' + e\}$, with co-kernels $\{\{c', d'\}, \{a', b'\}, 1\}$.

Consider now $u = a'c + a'd + b'd + e'$. Kernels of u are: $\{a' + b', c + d, a'c + a'd + b'd + e'\}$ with co-kernels $\{d, a', 1\}$.

The only kernel intersection is $p = a' + b'$. Thus:

$$z = p(c' + d') + e$$

$$u = dp + a'c + e'$$

The final network graph is shown in Figure 8.3.

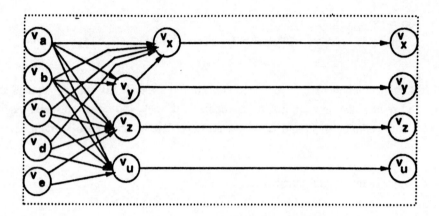

Figure 8.2: Modified logic network graph.

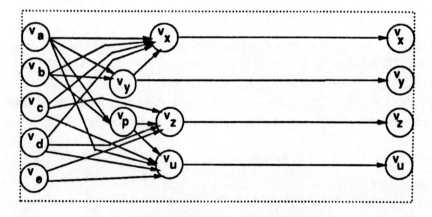

Figure 8.3: Final logic network graph.

8.5

Consider the logic network defined by the following expressions:

$$x = abcf + efc + de$$
$$y = acdef + def$$
$$z = bcd + acf$$

Determine the cube-variable matrix and all prime rectangles. Identify all feasible cube-intersections. Determine the minimum-literal network that can be derived by cube extraction.

Solution

	CUBE	ID	1 a	2 b	3 c	4 d	5 e	6 f
1	$abcf$	x	1	1	1	0	0	1
2	efc	x	0	0	1	0	1	1
3	de	x	0	0	0	1	1	0
4	$acdef$	y	1	0	1	1	1	1
5	def	y	0	0	0	1	1	1
6	bcd	z	0	1	1	1	0	0
7	acf	z	1	0	1	0	0	1

There are 15 prime rectangles:

$(\{1\}, \{1,2,3,6\}); (\{4\}, \{1,3,4,5,6\}); (\{6\}, \{2,3,4\});$
$(\{1,4,7\}, \{1,3,6\}); (\{1,6\}, \{2,3\}); (\{2,4\}, \{3,5,6\});$
$(\{3,4,5\}, \{4,5\}); (\{4,5\}, \{4,5,6\}); (\{4,6\}, \{3,4\});$
$(\{1,2,4,6,7\}, \{3\}); (\{1,2,4,7\}, \{3,6\}); (\{3,4,5,6\}, \{4\});$
$(\{2,3,4,5\}, \{5\}); (\{1,2,4,5,7\}, \{6\}); (\{2,4,5\}, \{5,6\});$

The cube intersections are all prime rectangles with more than one row. Thus, the first three rectangles should be discarded. Moreover, interesting cube intersection are those involving more than one expressions and having more than one variable. Thus we have restrict our attention to 7 prime rectangles:

$(\{1,4,7\}, \{1,3,6\}); (\{1,6\}, \{2,3\}); (\{2,4\}, \{3,5,6\});$
$(\{3,4,5\}, \{4,5\}); (\{4,6\}, \{3,4\});$
$(\{1,2,4,7\}, \{3,6\}); (\{2,4,5\}, \{5,6\});$

Note that the extraction of a cube may affect the extraction of another cube. Thus we select to prime rectangles with disjoint columns, namely: $(\{1,4,7\}, \{1,3,6\}); (\{3,4,5\}, \{4,5\})$ corresponding to extracting: acf and de.

The final minimal-literal network derived by cube extraction is shown in Figure 8.4.

The final network has 19 literals, thus reducing the literal count by 4.

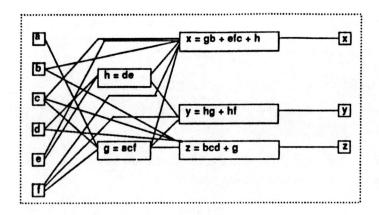

Figure 8.4: Final minimal-literal logic network.

8.6

Consider the logic network defined by the following expressions:

$$d = b'$$
$$f = (a + d)'$$
$$e = (ca)'$$
$$x = fe$$
$$y = d \oplus e$$

Inputs are $\{a, b, c\}$ and outputs are $\{x, y\}$. Assume $CDC_{in} = abc'$. Compute CDC_{out}.

Solution

We use the $CONTROLLABILITY$ algorithm of the textbook based on network cutsets. The cuts we use to calculate CDC_{out} are shown in Figure 8.5.

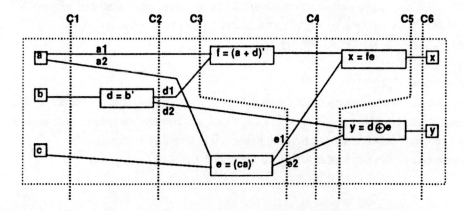

Figure 8.5: Logic network and cuts used for CDC calculations.

Given $CDC_{in} = abc'$, the algorithm proceeds as follows:

First cut $C1 = \{a, b, c\}$ and $v_x = d$.

$CDC_{cut} = abc' + d \oplus b' = abc' + db + d'b'$

Now b disappears:

$CDC_{cut} = CDC_{cut_b} CDC_{cut_{b'}} = ac'd'$

Second cut $C2 = \{a, c, d\}$ and $v_x = e$.

$CDC_{cut} = ac'd' + (ca)' \oplus e = ac'd' + ace + a'e' + c'e'$

Now c disappears:

$CDC_{cut} = CDC_{cut_c} CDC_{cut_{c'}} = ad'e + a'e'$

Third cut $C3 = \{a, d, e\}$ and $v_x = f$.

$CDC_{cut} = aed' + a'e' + f \oplus (a + d)' = ad'e + a'e' + af + fd + a'd'f'$

Now a disappears:

$CDC_{cut} = CDC_{cut_a} CDC_{cut_{a'}} = d'ef' + df + e'f$

Fourth cut $C4 = \{d, e, f\}$ and $v_x = x$.

$CDC_{cut} = ed'f' + df + e'f + x \oplus fe$

Now f disappears:

$CDC_{cut} = CDC_{cut_f} CDC_{cut_{f'}} = xd + xe' + x'd'e$

Fifth cut $C5 = \{d, e, x\}$ and $v_x = y$.

$CDC_{cut} = xd + xe' + x'd'e + y \oplus d \oplus e$

Now d and e disappear:

$CDC_{cut} = CDC_{cut_d} CDC_{cut_{d'}} = e'x + exy' + ex'y$

$CDC_{cut} = CDC_{cut_e} CDC_{cut_{e'}} = xy'$

The sixth cut corresponds to the output. Thus: $CDC_{out} = xy'$.

8.7

Consider the logic network of Problem 8.6. Compute the ODC sets for all internal and input vertices, assuming that the outputs are fully observable.

Solution

The ODCs of each output vertex are:

$$\text{ODC}_x = \begin{pmatrix} 0 \\ 1 \end{pmatrix} \quad ; \quad \text{ODC}_y = \begin{pmatrix} 1 \\ 0 \end{pmatrix}$$

$$\text{ODC}_f = \begin{pmatrix} 0 \\ 1 \end{pmatrix} + \begin{pmatrix} e' \\ e' \end{pmatrix} = \begin{pmatrix} e' \\ 1 \end{pmatrix}.$$

$$\text{ODC}_{e_1} = \begin{pmatrix} 0 \\ 1 \end{pmatrix} + \begin{pmatrix} f' \\ f' \end{pmatrix} = \begin{pmatrix} f' \\ 1 \end{pmatrix}.$$

$$\text{ODC}_{e_2} = \begin{pmatrix} 1 \\ 0 \end{pmatrix} + \begin{pmatrix} 0 \\ 0 \end{pmatrix} = \begin{pmatrix} 1 \\ 0 \end{pmatrix}.$$

$$\text{ODC}_e = \begin{pmatrix} f' \\ 1 \end{pmatrix} \overline{\oplus} \begin{pmatrix} 1 \\ 0 \end{pmatrix} = \begin{pmatrix} f' \\ 0 \end{pmatrix}.$$

$$\text{ODC}_c = \begin{pmatrix} f' \\ 0 \end{pmatrix} + \begin{pmatrix} a' \\ a' \end{pmatrix} = \begin{pmatrix} a' + f' \\ a' \end{pmatrix}.$$

$$\text{ODC}_{d_2} = \begin{pmatrix} 1 \\ 0 \end{pmatrix} + \begin{pmatrix} 0 \\ 0 \end{pmatrix} = \begin{pmatrix} 1 \\ 0 \end{pmatrix}.$$

$$\text{ODC}_{d_1} = \begin{pmatrix} e' \\ 1 \end{pmatrix} + \begin{pmatrix} a \\ a \end{pmatrix} = \begin{pmatrix} a + e' \\ 1 \end{pmatrix}.$$

$$\text{ODC}_{d} = \begin{pmatrix} a + e' \\ 1 \end{pmatrix} \overline{\oplus} \begin{pmatrix} 1 \\ 0 \end{pmatrix} = \begin{pmatrix} a' + e' \\ 0 \end{pmatrix}.$$

$$\text{ODC}_{b} = \begin{pmatrix} a' + e' \\ 0 \end{pmatrix} + \begin{pmatrix} 0 \\ 0 \end{pmatrix} = \begin{pmatrix} a' + e' \\ 0 \end{pmatrix}.$$

$$\text{ODC}_{a_1} = \begin{pmatrix} e' \\ 1 \end{pmatrix} + \begin{pmatrix} d \\ d \end{pmatrix} = \begin{pmatrix} e' + d \\ 1 \end{pmatrix} = \begin{pmatrix} ca + d \\ 1 \end{pmatrix}.$$

$$\text{ODC}_{a_2} = \begin{pmatrix} f' \\ 0 \end{pmatrix} + \begin{pmatrix} c' \\ c' \end{pmatrix} = \begin{pmatrix} f' + c' \\ c' \end{pmatrix} = \begin{pmatrix} a + d + c' \\ c' \end{pmatrix}.$$

$$\text{ODC}_{a} = \begin{pmatrix} ca + d \\ 1 \end{pmatrix}_{|a=a'} \overline{\oplus} \begin{pmatrix} a + d + c' \\ c' \end{pmatrix} = \begin{pmatrix} d \\ c' \end{pmatrix}.$$

8.8

Design an algorithm that computes the exact ODC set by backward traversal, that does not uses the results of Theorem 8.4.1, but that exploits formulae 8.9 and 8.10.

Solution

The basic idea is to replace any n-fanout point (with $n > 2$) by a binary tree of connections. This is equivalent to computing the vertex ODC by considering iteratively the contributions of two reconverging paths at a time. Thus it is possible to use formulae 8.9 and 8.10.

The following algorithm differs from the $OBSERVABILITY$ algorithm of the textbook only in the computation of the vertex ODC set.

```
OBSERVABILITY(G_n(V, E) , ODC_out) {
    foreach  vertex v_x ∈ V in reverse topological order {
        ODC_x = ODC_{y_1};                          /* set ODC to the ODC of the first successor */
        for (i = 1 to p - 1)                        /* consider all direct successors of v_x */
            ODC_x = ODC_x ⊕̄ ODC_{x,y_{i+1}}|_{y_{i+1}=y_{i+1}'};   /* apply two-way fanout formulae */
    }
}
```

Note that if $p = 1$, the inner for loop is not entered, and the vertex ODC equal the edge ODC.

8.9

Prove formally the following theorem justifying an exact filter. Consider a vertex v_x. Let $DC_x = D \cup E$ such that $|(sup(F) \cup sup(D)) \cap sup(E)| \leq 1$. Then, the cubes of E are useless for optimizing f_x.

Solution

The proof, reported by Reference 43 of the textbook, uses the following fact. Let C be the sum of two orthogonal functions, i.e. $C = A + B$ such that $sup(A) \cap sup(B) = \emptyset$. Let $p_A p_B$ be an implicant of C such that $sup(p_A) \subseteq sup(A)$ and $sup(p_B) \subseteq sup(B)$. Then, either $p_A \subseteq A$ or $p_B \subseteq B$.

Let us show the exactness of the filter. If $|(sup(F) \cup sup(D)) \cap sup(E)| < 1$, then the proof is trivial: none of the cubes of E can cover any portion of the cubes of F, and so the cubes of E are useless for optimizing f_x.

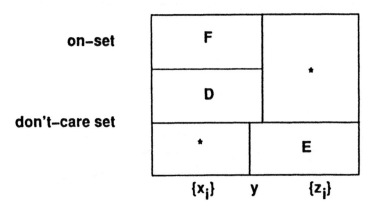

Figure 8.6: Special structure of incompletely specified function $(F, D + E)$.

If $|(sup(F) \cup sup(D)) \cap sup(E)| = 1$, then the structure of the function is illustrated in Figure 8.6. Note that F, D, and E all overlap in variable y; F and D have overlapping support in the variables $\{x_i\}$; and the cubes of E are the only cubes with support in the variables $\{z_i\}$.

So we have $sup(F + D) = \{x_i\} \cup \{y\}$ and $sup(E) = \{z_i\} \cup \{y\}$. All we need to prove is that for any prime p of F such that $sup(p) \cap \{z_i\} \neq \emptyset$, there is another prime q such that $sup(q) \cap \{z_i\} = \emptyset$ and any minterm of F covered by p is also covered by q.

Let $p = p_x p_y p_z$ where p_x, p_y, and p_z contain literals of p from $\{x_i\}$, y, and $\{z_i\}$ respectively. Since $p_x p_z = p_{p_y} \subseteq F_{p_y} + D_{p_y} + E_{p_y}$ and $sup(F_{p_y} + D_{p_y}) \cap sup(E_{p_y}) = \emptyset$, we have either $p_x \subseteq F_{p_y} + E_{p_y}$ or $p_z \subseteq E_{p_y}$ (by the aforementioned fact). If $p_x \subseteq F_{p_y} + E_{p_y}$, we have $p_x p_y \subseteq F + D$ which implies that for p to be prime $p_z = 1$. Hence, $p_x p_y = q \subseteq F + D$. In the other case ($p_z \subseteq E_{p_y}$) we have that for p to be prime $p_x = 1$. Hence $q = p_y p_z \subseteq E$, which contains irrelevant (i.e., *don't care*) information.

8.10

Give an example of the usefulness of an approximate filter based on the following. Discard those cubes of the *don't care* set whose support is disjoint from that of the function to be minimized. Show also that it is not an exact filter.

Solution

This filter can be justified by considering a matrix representation of the *don't care* set. Given a *don't care* set whose cubes can be organized as in the matrix shown in Figure 8.7, then all cubes in E are removed by this filter.

The rationale of the filter is that cubes in E are not directly related to the variables in F. For example consider: $f = ab' + a'b$ and a *don't care* cube c'. It is unlikely that such cube can help in minimizing f. On the other hand,

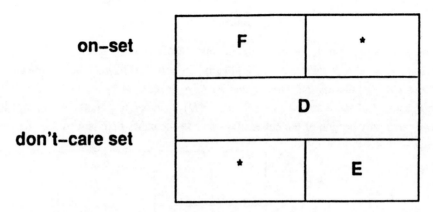

Figure 8.7: Special structure of incompletely specified function $(F, D + E)$.

the uselessness of cubes in E cannot be guaranteed in presence of other *don't care* cubes with support overlapping that of F and E. Consider again: $f = ab' + a'b$ and *don't care* cubes $abc + c'$. According to our matrix, the first *don't care* cube belongs to D and the second to E. In this case function f can be simplified to $\tilde{f} = a + b$.

8.11

Prove the following theorem. Let the input-output behavior of the network under consideration be represented by $\mathbf{f}$ and the corresponding external *don't care* set by $\mathbf{DC}_{ext}$. Let us apply simplification to vertex v_x and let g_x be a feasible implementation of the corresponding local function. Then:

$$(\mathbf{f}_{min} \cap \mathbf{f}'|_{x=0}) \cup (\mathbf{f}'_{max} \cap \mathbf{f}|_{x=0}) \subseteq g_x 1 \subseteq (\mathbf{f}_{max} \cup \mathbf{f}'|_{x=1}) \cap (\mathbf{f}'_{min} \cup \mathbf{f}|_{x=1})$$

where $\mathbf{f}_{min} = (\mathbf{f} \cap \mathbf{DC}'_{ext})$ and $\mathbf{f}_{max} = (\mathbf{f} \cup \mathbf{DC}_{ext})$.

Solution

First of all, note that with $\mathbf{f}_{min}$ and $\mathbf{f}_{max}$ defined as above, we have

$$\mathbf{f}_{min} \subseteq \mathbf{f} \subseteq \mathbf{f}_{max} \tag{8.1}$$

Now $\mathbf{f}$ can be expressed in terms of the signal x:

$$\mathbf{f} = \mathbf{f}(\mathbf{y}, x) = x'\mathbf{f}|_{x=0} \cup x\mathbf{f}|_{x=1} = (x1 \cup \mathbf{f}|_{x=0}) \cap (x'1 \cup \mathbf{f}|_{x=1}) \tag{8.2}$$

By replacing Eq. (8.2) in Eq. (8.1), it follows that x must satisfy:

$$\mathbf{f}_{min} \subseteq x'\mathbf{f}|_{x=0} \cup x\mathbf{f}|_{x=1} \subseteq \mathbf{f}_{max} \tag{8.3}$$

The upper bound in Eq. (8.3) holds if and only if $x'\mathbf{f}|_{x=0} \subseteq \mathbf{f}_{max}$ and $x\mathbf{f}|_{x=1} \subseteq \mathbf{f}_{max}$, i.e.

$$x'1 \subseteq \mathbf{f}_{max} \cup \mathbf{f}'|_{x=0}; \quad x1 \subseteq \mathbf{f}_{max} \cup \mathbf{f}'|_{x=1} \tag{8.4}$$

Eq. (8.4) can be rewritten as

$$\mathbf{f'_{max}} \cap \mathbf{f}|_{x=0} \subseteq x1 \subseteq \mathbf{f_{max}} \cup \mathbf{f'}|_{x=1} \tag{8.5}$$

Similarly, the lower bound in Eq. (8.3) holds if and only if $\mathbf{f}_{x'} \cup x1 \supseteq \mathbf{f_{min}}$ and $\mathbf{f}_x \cup x'1 \supseteq \mathbf{f_{min}}$, i.e.

$$\mathbf{f_{min}} \cap \mathbf{f}|_{x=0} \subseteq x1 \subseteq \mathbf{f'_{min}} \cup \mathbf{f}|_{x=1} \tag{8.6}$$

Eq. (8.5) and (8.6) can be merged together, to obtain:

$$(\mathbf{f_{min}} \cap \mathbf{f'}|_{x=0}) \cup (\mathbf{f'_{max}} \cap \mathbf{f}|_{x=0}) \subseteq x1 \subseteq (\mathbf{f_{max}} \cup \mathbf{f}|_{x=1}) \cap (\mathbf{f'_{min}} \cup \mathbf{f}|_{x=1}) \tag{8.7}$$

Eq. (8.7) represents the exact degrees of freedom available in the synthesis of the expression g_x for variable x.

8.12

Derive a recursive formula to compute the controlling set $C_{11}(x)$. Justify the formula.

Solution

We assume that the all local functions in the network are NORS . Consider the conditions that apply when a variable $x = 1$ forces $s = 1$.

First, a signal s is forced to 1 by $x = 1$ if s is an input to f_y (NOR) with output y that is forced to 0 by $x = 1$ and such that all other inputs to f_y (other than s) are also forced to 0 by $x = 1$. Indeed, input s of the NOR has to be 1 for its output to be 0, since all other inputs are 0.

Second, if $x = 1$ forces all variables in the support of f_y to 0, then it forces y to 1 (NOR output). Eventually, $x \in C_{11}(x)$. Hence the controlling set can be defined recursively as follows:

$$C_{11}(x) = \{s \in S : \exists y \in C_{10}(x) \text{ and } \forall t \in p(y), t \neq s, t \in C_{10}(x)\} \cup \{s \in S : \forall y \in p(s); y \in C_{10}(x)\} \cup \{x\} \cup C_{11}(x)$$

8.13

Design an exact algorithm for inverter minimization in a tree-structured network. Determine its time complexity.

Solution

We describe a dynamic programming algorithm for inverter minimization in a tree-structured network, taken from Reference 43. Given a tree network N, let $ROOT(N)$ be the root vertex of N. Let N_v be the network rooted at vertex v. Let $NI(N)$ be the number of inverters in the network N. A polarity assignment of N is represented by function: $P(N)$ which assigns to each vertex a binary value: a 1 if the vertex is inverted and assigned to the complemented local function, a 0 otherwise. $NFO(v)$ and $PFO(v)$ are as defined in the text (Section 8.4.3). $FI(v)$ denotes the predecessors (children) of vertex v and $PI(N)$ the primary inputs.

The algorithm has two major components: $OPA\_I(N)$ finds the optimum polarity assignment of N with an inverter in front of the root vertex $ROOT(N)$, while $OPA\_N(N)$ finds the optimum polarity assignment with no inverter in front of $ROOT(N)$. The two components are described as two co-routines: each one calls itself or the other with a smaller tree, and terminates at the primary inputs of N.

```
OPA_N(N){
     P = {(ROOT(N),0)}
     for each v ∈ FI(ROOT(N)) and v ∉ PI(N) {
          if (ROOT(N) ∈ PFO(f)) {
               if (NI(OPA_N(N_v)) < NI(OPA_I(N_v)))
                    P = P ∪ OPA_N(N_v);
               else
                    P = P ∪ OPA_I(N_v);
          }
          else
               if (NI(OPA_N(N_v)) + 1 < NI(OPA_I(N_v)) − 1)
                    P = P ∪ OPA_N(N_v);
               else
                    P = P ∪ OPA_I(N_v);
          }
     }
     return(P);
}
```

$OPA\_I(N)$ is very similar to $OPA\_N(N)$. It assigns "1" to the root and inverts the dependencies of the root on its predecessors.

```
OPA_I(N){
     P = {(ROOT(N),1)}
     for each v ∈ FI(ROOT(N)) and v ∉ PI(N) {
          if (ROOT(N) ∈ NFO(v))
               if (NI(OPA_N(N_v)) < NI(OPA_I(N_v)))
                    P = P ∪ OPA_N(N_v);
               else
                    P = P ∪ OPA_I(N_v);
          }
          else
               if (NI(OPA_N(N_v)) + 1 < NI(OPA_I(N_v)) − 1)
                    P = P ∪ OPA_N(N_v);
               else
                    P = P ∪ OPA_I(N_v);
          }
     }
     return(P);
}
```

Now, to find the optimum polarity assignment of a tree network, algorithm OPA simply evaluates the results of OPA_N and OPA_I and picks the better one.

```
OPA(N){
    if (NI(OPA_N(N)) < NI(OPA_I(N)))
        return(OPA_N(N));
    else
        return(OPA_I(N));
}
```

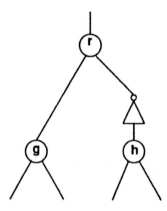

Figure 8.8: Finding $OPA\_N(N_r)$ and $OPA\_I(N_r)$.

We give a simple example of the execution of the algorithm on the network of Figure 8.8. Vertex r is the current root with two predecessors g and h, and r depends on the positive polarity of g and the negative polarity of h (i.e. on h'). To find $OPA\_N(N_r)$, r must not be flipped. Since r depends on the positive polarity of g, the optimum polarity assignment of N_g should be used. This is found by comparing $NI(OPA\_N(N_g))$ with $NI(OPA\_I(N_g))$. If r depends on the negative polarity of an input, e.g. h, then the number of inverters from this branch is either $NI(OPA\_N(N_h)) + 1$ or $NI(OPA\_I(N_h)) - 1$. This justifies the last "if" statement of the algorithm.

Algorithm OPA, based on dynamic programming, has complexity $O(|N|)$ where $|N|$ is the number of vertex in the tree network. This can be easily seen in the example since each vertex in the network is processed exactly twice, once by OPA_N and once by OPA_I. Each time, a fixed amount of operations is performed. In particular, since the polarity assignment of sub-trees is independent of each other, the union operation in the algorithm OPA_N and OPA_I can be done in constant time.

8.14

Formulate the inverter minimization problem as a ZOLP. Consider networks with general topology.

Solution

The ZOLP problem is set up as follows. Each of the primary inputs and internal signals (denoted by S) is associated with a binary variable in the set X, where a value of 1 implies the presence of an inverter to provide the negative polarity of the signals. Moreover, each internal vertex is associated with an additional binary variable in set Y whose value being 1 implies that the local function is replaced by its complement. The objective is to minimize the sum of all variables associated with the signals:

$$\sum_{s \in S} x_s$$

Constraints are used to ensure the consistency of the network. Let x be a primary input or an internal vertex. $NFO(x)$ contains all successors of x which presently depend on the negative polarity of x. $PFO(x)$ contains all the successors of x which presently depend on the positive polarity of x. (This is consistent with the textbook's definition of $NFO(f)$ and $PFO(f)$; it is just stated in a different way).

The inverter can be eliminated if all vertices in $NFO(x)$ are complemented. In addition, if x is an internal vertex, the inverter can also be eliminated by complementing all vertices in $PFO(x)$ and x. These are the basis for deriving the constraints. It is worth mentioning that at the presence of the inverter, the constraint associated with x should be automatically satisfied simply because both polarity of x are available for the successors of xf to use.

Namely the constraints are:

$$(1 - x_s)(\sum_{t \in FO(s)} z_s^t + N_s y_f - N_s) = 0 \quad f \notin PI(N)$$
$$(1 - x_s)(\sum_{t \in FO(s)} z_s^t - N_s) = 0 \qquad\quad s \in PI(N)$$

where $FO(s)$ are the successors of s, $N_s = |FO(s)|$ and z_s^t is defined as

$$z_s^t = \begin{cases} 1 - y_t & y \in PFO(N) \\ y_t & y \in NFO(N) \end{cases}$$

More details and an example are reported in Reference 43.

8.15

Consider the logic network defined by the following expressions:

$$
\begin{aligned}
k &= a' \\
e &= k + b \\
g &= (b + c)' \\
f &= ag \\
h &= ab \\
i &= f \overline{\oplus} d \\
j &= d + s \\
x &= e \oplus i \\
y &= j + h
\end{aligned}
$$

Inputs are $\{a, b, c, d, s\}$ and outputs are $\{x, y\}$. Draw the logic network graph. Assume that the delay of each inverter, AND and OR gates is 1 and that the delay of each NOR , EXOR and EXNOR gate is 2, compute the data-ready and slacks for all vertices in the network. Assume that the input data-ready times are zero except for $t_s = 4$ and that the required data-ready time at the outputs is 7. Determine the topological critical path.

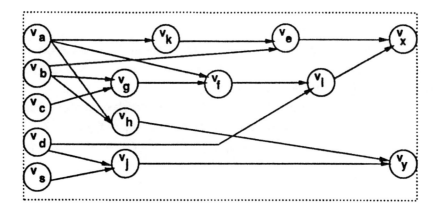

Figure 8.9: Logic network graph for problem 8.15.

Solution

The logic network graph is shown in Figure 8.9. The data-ready times, required data-ready times and slacks are listed in the following table.

Vertex	Data-ready time	Required data-ready time	Slack
a	0	2	2
b	0	0	0
c	0	0	0
d	0	3	3
e	2	5	3
f	3	3	0
g	2	2	0
h	1	6	5
i	5	5	0
j	5	6	1
k	1	4	3
s	4	5	1
x	7	7	0
y	6	7	1

The topological critical paths of the circuit are $(v_b, v_g, v_f, v_i, v_x)$ and $(v_c, v_g, v_f, v_i, v_x)$.

8.16

Consider the circuit of Figure 8.31. Is it fully testable for single stuck-at faults? Can you draw the conclusion that a critical true path is not statically sensitizable if the circuit is not fully testable? Why?

Solution

The circuit of Figure 8.31 (of the textbook) is not fully testable for single stuck-at faults. Consider for example the test for d stuck-at 0. Such a test requires setting $d = 1$ and thus $a = b = 1$. Under this condition, $e = 0$ and the effects of d possibly being stuck is not observable at the primary output o which stays at 0.

On the other hand, a critical true path may still not be statically sensitizable even if the circuit is fully testable. Consider for example adding a primary output corresponding to d to the circuit of Figure 8.31. The modified circuit is now fully testable, but paths $\{(v_a, v_d, v_g, v_o); (v_b, v_d, v_g, v_o)\}$ are still not statically sensitizable.

Chapter 9

Sequential Logic Optimization

9.1

Consider the state table of Example 9.2.3. Derive a completely specified cover by replacing the *don't care* entries by 0s. Minimize the machine using the standard and Hopcroft algorithms. Repeat the exercise with the *don't care* entries replaced by 0 and 1.

Solution

Let the *don't care* entries be 0s. Then the state table is as follows:

INPUT	STATE	N-STATE	OUTPUT
0	s_1	s_3	1
1	s_1	s_5	0
0	s_2	s_3	0
1	s_2	s_5	1
0	s_3	s_2	0
1	s_3	s_1	1
0	s_4	s_4	0
1	s_4	s_5	1
0	s_5	s_4	1
1	s_5	s_1	0

The state set can be partitioned first according to the outputs, i.e.

$$\Pi_1 = \{\{s_1, s_5\}, \{s_2, s_3, s_4\}\}$$

Then we check each block of Π_1, to see if the corresponding next-states are in a single block of Π_1 for any input. The next-states of s_1 and s_5 are in the same blocks for any input. The same applies to states s_2, s_3, s_4. Hence Π_1 represents a partition into equivalent state sets. The corresponding state diagram is shown in Figure 9.5 (b) of the textbook.

Let us use Hopcroft's algorithm. The state set can be partitioned first according to the outputs, as in the previous case.

$$\Pi_1 = \{\{s_1, s_5\}, \{s_2, s_3, s_4\}\} = \{A_1, A_2\}$$

Then we check each block of Π_1. Consider A_1 first. For input $i = 0$, the subset P of the states whose next state are in A_1 is void. For input $i = 1$, the subset P of the states whose next state are in A_1 is the entire state set S. Then A_2 is consistent with A_1.

Consider A_2 next. For input $i = 0$, the subset P of the states whose next state are in A_2 is the entire state set S. For input $i = 1$, the subset P of the states whose next state are in A_2 is void. Then A_1 is consistent with A_2. Thus Π_1 represents a partition into equivalent state sets.

Let the *don't care* entries be 0 and 1. Then the state table is as follows:

INPUT	STATE	N-STATE	OUTPUT
0	s_1	s_3	1
1	s_1	s_5	0
0	s_2	s_3	1
1	s_2	s_5	1
0	s_3	s_2	0
1	s_3	s_1	1
0	s_4	s_4	0
1	s_4	s_5	1
0	s_5	s_4	1
1	s_5	s_1	0

The state set can be partitioned first according to the outputs, i.e.

$$\Pi_1 = \{\{s_1, s_5\}, \{s_2\}, \{s_3, s_4\}\}$$

Then we check each block of Π_1, to see if the corresponding next-states are in a single block of Π_1 for any input. The next-states of s_1 and s_5 are in the same blocks for any input, but the next-states of s_3 and s_4 are not. Thus we split the block $\{s_3, s_4\}$ and we get:

$$\Pi_2 = \{\{s_1, s_5\}, \{s_2\}, \{s_3\}, \{s_4\}\}$$

Now the next states of s_1 and s_5 are no longer in the same blocks for any input, and therefore we have to split the block $\{s_1, s_5\}$. We obtain then the 0-partition:

$$\Pi_3 = \{\{s_1\}, \{s_5\}, \{s_2\}, \{s_3\}, \{s_4\}\}$$

Let us use Hopcroft's algorithm. The state set can be partitioned first according to the outputs, as in the previous case.

$$\Pi_1 = \{\{s_1, s_5\}, \{s_2\}, \{s_3, s_4\}\} = \{A_1, A_2, A_3\}$$

Then we check each block of Π_1. Consider A_1 first. For input $i = 0$, the subset P of the states whose next state are in A_1 is void. For input $i = 1$, the subset P of the states whose next state are in A_1 is the entire state set S. Then A_2 and A_3 are consistent with A_1.

Consider A_2 next. For input $i = 0$, the subset P of the states whose next state are in A_3 is $P = \{s_3\}$. For input $i = 1$, the subset P of the states whose next state are in A_2 is void.

Since $P \cap A_3 \neq \emptyset$, A_3 must be split and we have the following partition:

$$\Pi_2 = \{\{s_1, s_5\}, \{s_2\}, \{s_3\}, \{s_4\}\} = \{A_1, A_2, A_{31}, A_{32}\}$$

We consider then A_{31}. For input $i = 0$, the subset P of the states whose next state are in A_{31} is $P = \{s_1, s_2\}$
For input $i = 1$, the subset P of the states whose next state are in A_{31} is void.

Since $P \cap A_1 \neq \emptyset$, A_1 must be split and we have the 0 partition:

$$\Pi_3 = \{\{s_1\}, \{s_5\}, \{s_2\}, \{s_3\}, \{s_4\}\}$$

9.2

Consider the state table of Example 9.2.3. Derive a minimum symbolic cover and the corresponding encoding constraints. Compute then a feasible encoding. Can you reduce the encoding length by using constraints derived from a non-minimum cover? Show possible product-term/encoding-length trade-off.

Solution

The original table is:

INPUT	STATE	N-STATE	OUTPUT
0	s_1	s_3	1
1	s_1	s_5	*
0	s_2	s_3	*
1	s_2	s_5	1
0	s_3	s_2	0
1	s_3	s_1	1
0	s_4	s_4	0
1	s_4	s_5	1
0	s_5	s_4	1
1	s_5	s_1	0

A simple reduction yields:

INPUT	STATE	N-STATE	OUTPUT
0	s_1, s_2	s_3	1
1	s_1, s_2, s_4	s_5	1
0	s_3	s_2	0
1	s_3	s_1	1
0	s_4	s_4	0
0	s_5	s_4	1
1	s_5	s_1	0

A feasible encoding should satisfy only input constraints, specified by:

$$A = \begin{bmatrix} 1 & 1 & 0 & 0 & 0 \\ 1 & 1 & 0 & 1 & 0 \end{bmatrix}$$

A valid encoding is:

$$E = \begin{bmatrix} 1 & 0 & 0 \\ 0 & 0 & 0 \\ 0 & 0 & 1 \\ 0 & 1 & 0 \\ 1 & 0 & 1 \end{bmatrix}$$

An encoded cover is:

0	*00	001	1
1	**0	101	1
1	001	100	1
0	010	010	0
0	101	010	1
1	101	100	0

Note that the implicant corresponding to next state s_2 can be dropped. The cover has 6 rows and 8 columns. Let us consider next a minimal symbolic cover.

INPUT	STATE	N-STATE	OUTPUT
0	s_1, s_2, s_5	s_3	1
1	s_1, s_2, s_4, s_3	s_5	1
0	s_3	s_2	0
1	s_3, s_5	s_1	0
0	s_4, s_5	s_4	0

Under the conditions that s_1 covers s_5 and s_4 covers s_3. Thus:

$$A = \begin{bmatrix} 1 & 1 & 0 & 0 & 1 \\ 1 & 1 & 1 & 1 & 0 \\ 0 & 0 & 1 & 0 & 1 \\ 0 & 0 & 0 & 1 & 1 \end{bmatrix} \qquad B = \begin{bmatrix} 0 & 0 & 0 & 0 & 1 \\ 0 & 0 & 0 & 0 & 0 \\ 0 & 0 & 0 & 0 & 0 \\ 0 & 0 & 1 & 0 & 0 \\ 0 & 0 & 0 & 0 & 0 \end{bmatrix}$$

Note that a cover with the additional constraint that s_2 is covered by all other states (and thus s_2 could be encoded by a string of 0s and the implicant with next state s_2 be dropped) has no feasible encoding, as shown by the theorem of Problem 9.2. Indeed, the following covering relation $s_1 > s_5 > s_2$ would conflict with constraint expressed by the second row of A.

An encoding satisfying the constraints is:

$$E = \begin{bmatrix} 1 & 1 & 1 & 1 & 1 \\ 1 & 1 & 1 & 0 & 0 \\ 1 & 0 & 0 & 0 & 0 \\ 1 & 0 & 1 & 1 & 0 \\ 0 & 1 & 0 & 1 & 0 \end{bmatrix}$$

An encoded cover requires 5 rows and 12 columns. Other intermediate solutions can be obtained by renouncing the merger of some implicants.

9.3

Consider the state encoding problem specified by two matrices A and B derived by symbolic minimization. Assume that matrix B specifies only covering constraints (i.e. exclude disjunctive relations). Let S be the state set. Prove the following. A necessary and sufficient condition for the existence of an encoding of S satisfying both the constraints specified by A and B is that for each triple of states $\{r, s, t\} \subseteq S$ such that $b_{rs} = 1$ and $b_{st} = 1$ there exist no row k of A such that $a_{kr} = 1, a_{ks} = 0, a_{kt} = 1$.

Solution

Necessity. For the sake of contradiction, suppose there exists an encoding matrix E satisfying both the input and the output constraint relation and suppose that $b_{rs} = b_{st} = 1$ and for some $k, 1 \le k \le n_s, a_{kr} = 1, a_{ks} = 0$ and $a_{kt} = 1$. Let $J_{rt} = \{j : e_{rj} = 1 \text{ and } e_{tj} = 0\}$ and $J_{st} = \{j : e_{sj} = 1 \text{ and } e_{tj} = 0\}$. Since by assumption the encoding of r covers the encoding of s which covers the encoding of t, then $J_{rt} \subset J_{st}$. Let α be the supercube of the codes of the states with a 1 in constraint (row) k of A . Then α is such that $\alpha_j = *$ if $j \in J_{rt}$ and either $\alpha_j = *$ or $\alpha_j = e_{tj}$ if $j \notin J_{rt}$. Since $e_{sj} = e_{tj} \ \forall j \notin J_{st}$ and $\alpha_j = * \ \forall j \in J_{st}$ then the constraint represented by row k of A is not satisfied and we have a contradiction.

Sufficiency. Recall that $\tilde{E} = A^T$ satisfies the input constraint relation. Let E be a matrix constructed as follows. For each column k of $\tilde{E}$, let:

$$J_k^0 = \{j : \tilde{e}_{jk} = 0 \text{ and } \exists x : \tilde{e}_{xk} = 1 \text{ and } b_{xj} = 1\}$$

$$J_k^1 = \{j : \tilde{e}_{jk} = 0 \text{ and } \exists x : \tilde{e}_{xk} = 1 \text{ and } b_{jx} = 1\}$$

The set $J_k^0 (J_k^1)$ is the set of words with a 0 encoding in column k of $\tilde{E}$ and required to be covered by (to cover) some words with a 1 encoding in column k of $\tilde{E}$. Note that by assumption $J_k^0 \cap J_k^1 = \emptyset$. Let us now construct E. Column k of E is:

$$\begin{cases} \text{column } k \text{ of } \tilde{E} & \text{if } J_k^1 = \emptyset \\ \text{column } k \text{ of } \tilde{E} \text{ complemented} & \text{if } J_k^1 \ne \emptyset \text{ and } J_k^0 = \emptyset \\ T & \text{otherwise} \end{cases}$$

where T is a column vector whose entries are bit-pairs:

$$t_j = \begin{cases} 01 & \forall j : \tilde{e}_{jk} = 1 \\ 11 & \forall j \in J_k^1 \\ 00 & \text{else} \end{cases}$$

Then column k of E (which may become a column pair) satisfies the output constraint relation. Since the encoding matrix E is obtained from $\tilde{E}$ by replacing some columns by their complement or by a two-bit encoding of their entries, then the encoding matrix E satisfies the input constraint relation. Moreover, since the covering relations are satisfied for each column by construction, then also the entire encoding matrix E satisfies the output constraint relation.

9.4

Consider the network of Figure 9.8. Draw the weighted graph modeling the search for a legal retiming with cycle-time of 22 units using the Bellman-Ford method. Compute the retiming and draw the retimed network graph.

Solution

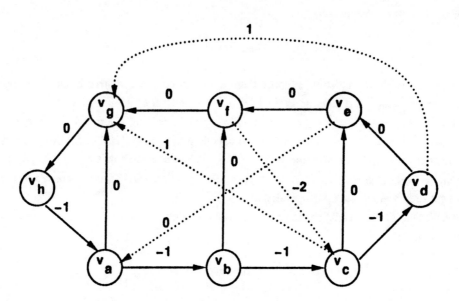

Figure 9.1: Constraint graph.

The algorithm first computes Inequalities 9.4 (of the textbook), which can be represented by a graph with the same topology of the network and complementing the weights. (Because $r_i - r_j \leq w_{ij}$ implies $r_j \geq r_i - w_{ij}$ for each edge $(v_i, v_j) \in E$.) This is shown by the solid edges of Figure 9.1.

For this problem we select $\phi = 22$. Then Inequalities 9.5 are constructed. We note that $D(v_a, v_i) < 22 \; \forall v_i \in \{v_b, v_c, v_d, v_e, v_f, v_g\}$. Similarly, $D(v_b, v_i) < 22 \; \forall v_i \in \{v_h, v_a, v_d, v_e, v_f, v_g\}$. However, for v_c, $D(v_c, v_g) = 24$, which is a violation. So we have the inequality $r_c - r_g \leq W(v_c, v_g) - 1 \Rightarrow r_c - r_g \leq -1$ which implies a constraint from v_c to v_g of weight 1. (Note that other edges with tail in v_c are superfluous.)

For v_d, $D(v_d, v_g) = 24$, which is a violation. So as before we have the inequality $r_d - r_g \leq W(v_d, v_g) - 1$ which implies a constraint from v_d to v_g of weight 1.

For v_e, $D(v_e, v_a) = 24$, which is a violation. So again we have the inequality $r_e - r_a \leq W(v_e, v_a) - 1$ which implies a constraint from v_e to v_a of weight 0.

Finally, for v_f, $D(v_f, v_c) = 23$, which is a violation. The inequality $r_f - r_c \leq W(v_f, v_c) - 1$ which implies a constraint from v_f to v_c of weight -2.

There are no other violations for v_f, v_g, v_h. The final constraint graph is shown in Figure 9.1.

An inspection of the graph shows no positive cycle, and therefore the constraints are consistent. The Bellman-Ford algorithm can be used to compute the retiming vector. The retiming entries can be thought of as the weights of the longest path from a reference vertex, say v_h, with $r_h = 0$. In this case the retiming vector is $-[1234321]^T$. Note that the solution is not unique, and that other (larger) retiming values are possible. The retimed graph is shown in Figure 9.2. The longest path has delay $16 < 22 = \phi$.

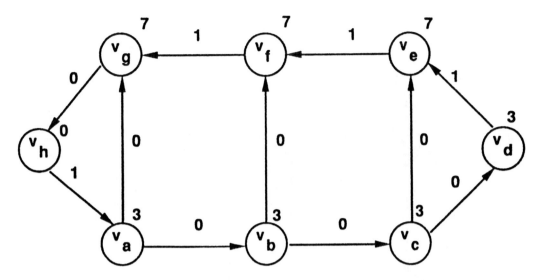

Figure 9.2: Retimed network.

9.5

Suppose you want to constrain the maximum number of registers on a path while doing retiming. How do you incorporate this requirement in the retiming formalism ? Would the complexity of the algorithm be affected ? As an example, assume that you require at most one registers on the path (v_d, v_h) in the network of Figure 9.8. What would the minimum cycle-time be? Show graphically the constraints of the Bellman-Ford algorithm in correspondence with the minimum cycle-time as well as the retimed network graph.

Solution

We wish to incorporate the requirement of a maximum number of registers between two vertices v_i and v_j of the graph into the retiming formalism. Recall that the number of registers on a path after retiming is: $\tilde{w}(v_i, \ldots, v_j) = w(v_i, \ldots, v_j) + r_j - r_i$ Then, the following set of equations for retiming accomplishes the desired goal:

Minimize cycle-time ϕ, subject to:

$$r_i - r_j \leq w_{ij} \qquad \forall (v_i, v_j) \in E$$
$$r_i - r_j \leq W(v_i, v_j) - 1 \quad \forall v_i, v_j : D(v_i, v_j) > \phi$$
$$r_j - r_i \leq M_{ij} - m_{ij} \qquad \forall v_i, v_j \text{ where an upper bound is specified}$$

where $M_{ij} =$ is the maximum allowed number of registers between v_i and v_j and $m_{ij} =$ is the maximum number of registers on any path between v_i and v_j before retiming.

The overall worst-case computational complexity is still $O(|V|^3 log|V|)$ for the following reasons:

- The computation of **D** and **W** is not affected.

- The existence of a feasible retiming for a given cycle time requires still solving a set of linear inequalities, and thus the complexity is similar to that of the Bellman-Ford algorithm.

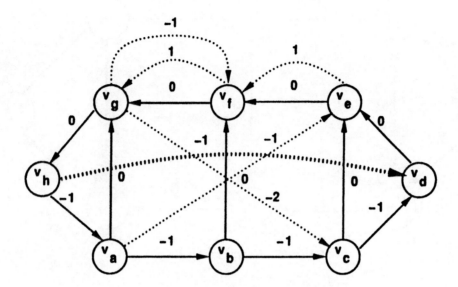

Figure 9.3: Constraint graph for $\phi = 13$

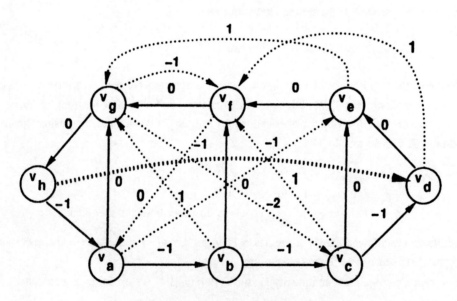

Figure 9.4: Constraint graph for $\phi = 14$

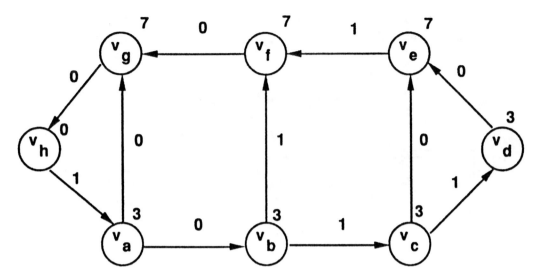

Figure 9.5: Retimed network graph.

As an example, we require at most one registers on the path (v_d, v_h), which originally had zero registers. Thus the corresponding constraint is: $r_h - r_d \leq 1 - 0$

The constraint graph for $\phi = 13$ is shown in Figure 9.3. Note that it has a positive cycle, and no feasible solution exists with $\phi = 13$ and the specified maximum delay constraint.

The constraint graph for $\phi = 14$ is shown in Figure 9.4. There are no positive cycles. A feasible solution is shown in Figure 9.5.

9.6

Give examples of synchronous substitution and elimination as applied to the network of Figure 9.7.

Solution

An example of algebraic substitution is shown in Figure 9.6, by noticing that $b = a@1$.

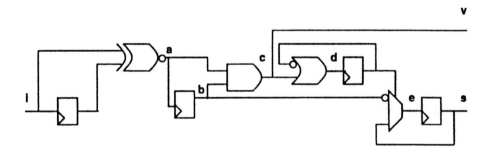

Figure 9.6: Algebraic substitution.

An example of a synchronous elimination is shown in Figure 9.7. The new gate implements the following function: $c = ab = aa@1 = (ii@1 + i'i@1')(i@1i@2 + i@1'i@2') = ii@1i@2 + i'i@1'i@2'$

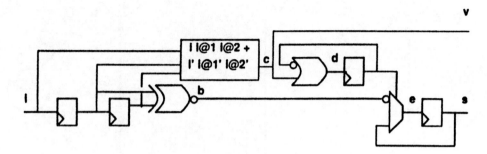

Figure 9.7: Synchronous elimination.

9.7

Show that for a pipelined network, for any single perturbation at any vertex v_x representing the replacement of a local function f_x by g_x, necessary and sufficient conditions for the feasibility of the replacement are:

$$\delta^{(n-p)}1 \subseteq \mathbf{ODC}^{(n)}_{x(n-p)} + \mathbf{DC}^{(n)}_{ext} \quad \forall n \geq 0 \tag{9.1}$$

for a suitable value of p.

Solution

In a generic acyclic synchronous logic network, when replacing f_x by g_x, $\mathbf{e}^{(n)} = \mathbf{f}^x(\delta^{(n)}, \ldots, \delta^{(n-p)}) \oplus \mathbf{f}^x(0, \ldots, 0)$ represents the error introduced in the circuit, as measured at the output at time n.

On the other hand, for a pipelined networks, all paths from any vertex to any output have the same weight. Assume such weight is p for the vertex v_x under consideration. Thus the error is $\mathbf{e}^{(n)} = \mathbf{f}^x(\delta^{(n-p)}) \oplus \mathbf{f}^x(0)$. In simple terms, the perturbation can be seen as a single perturbation localized in time and not as a sequence of perturbations. As a consequence, we can apply the formalism for single-vertex perturbation of Chapter 8.

Assume the replacement is feasible, i.e. $\mathbf{e}^{(n)} \subseteq \mathbf{DC}^{(n)}_{ext}$. Since $\mathbf{e}^{(n)} = \mathbf{f}^x(\delta^{(n-p)}) \oplus \mathbf{f}^x(0)$, by performing an expansion on variable $\delta^{(n-p)}$ we have:

$$\mathbf{e}^{(n)} = \delta^{(n-p)}(\mathbf{f}^x(0) \oplus \mathbf{f}^x(1)) + \delta'^{(n-p)}(\mathbf{f}^x(0) \oplus \mathbf{f}^x(0))$$

Hence: $\mathbf{e}^{(n)} = \delta^{(n-p)} \mathbf{ODC}'^{(n)}_{x(n-p)}$ which implies that:

$$\delta^{(n-p)}\mathbf{ODC}'^{(n)}_{x(n-p)} \subseteq \mathbf{DC}_{ext} \tag{9.2}$$

The above equality holds if and only if:

$$\delta^{(n-p)}1 \subseteq \mathbf{DC}_{ext} + \mathbf{ODC}^{(n)}_{x(n-p)} \tag{9.3}$$

If we assume that $sup(f_x)$ and $sup(g_x)$ are primary inputs, then the condition is also necessary for equivalence.

9.8

Consider the acyclic synchronous logic network obtained from that of Figure 9.7 (a) by cutting the loops and using additional input variables for the dangling connections. Determine the observability *don't care* sets at all internal and input vertices.

Solution

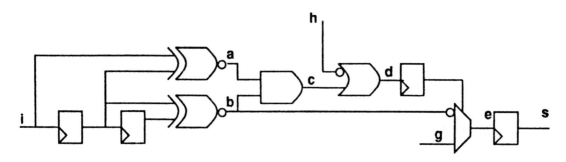

Figure 9.8: Synchronous elimination.

The modified logic network (with loops cut) is shown in Figure 9.8. We consider only one output, namely s, because output $v = c$. Thus we use the scalar notation.

We compute the ODC sets by backward traversal. Note that vertex v_b is observable at the output through two paths of different weight, that are thus independent from each other. Let $f = gb + g'b'$. Then:

$$\begin{aligned}
ODC_{g(n)} &= ODC_{g(n)}^{(n+1)} = d'^{(n-1)} \\
& ODC_{b(n)}^{(n+1)} = d^{(n-1)} \\
ODC_{d(n)} &= ODC_{d(n)}^{(n+2)} = f^{(n+1)} \\
ODC_{c(n)} &= ODC_{c(n)}^{(n+2)} = h'^{(n)} + f^{(n+1)} \\
&= ODC_{b(n)}^{(n+2)} = a'^{(n)} + h'^{(n)} + f^{(n+1)} \\
ODC_{b(n)} &= ODC_{b(n)}^{(n+1)} ODC_{b(n)}^{(n+2)} = d^{(n-1)}(a'^{(n)} + h'^{(n)} + f^{(n+1)}) \\
ODC_{a(n)} &= ODC_{a(n)}^{(n+2)} = b'^{(n)} + h'^{(n)} + f^{(n+1)} \\
& ODC_{i(n)}^{(n+2)} = ODC_{a(n)}^{(n+2)} \\
& ODC_{i(n-1)}^{(n+2)} = ODC_{a(n)}^{(n+2)} \;\overline{\oplus}\; ODC_{b(n)}^{(n+2)}|a = a' \\
& ODC_{i(n-2)}^{(n+2)} = ODC_{b(n)}^{(n+2)}
\end{aligned}$$

Chapter 10

Cell-library binding

10.1

Consider the binding of a network implementing the conjunction of 10 variables. Available cells are only two-input AND gates with cost 2, three-input AND gates with cost 3 and four-input AND gates with cost 4. Find an optimum cover of a balanced tree decomposition of the network using two-input AND gates as base functions. Is this the best implementation of the given network with the available cells? Is there another decomposition into the same base-function leading to a lower cost solution?

Solution

A balanced decomposition with two-input AND gates as base functions is shown in Figure 10.1 (a). An optimum cover (for this decomposition) is also shown in Figure 10.1 (a). It employs 3 three-input ANDs and 1 four-input AND , with a total cost of 3*3+1*4 =13.

The binding of Figure 10.1 (a) is not the best way of implementing the specified network with the given gates. Indeed, a better implementation is shown in Figure 10.1 (b), requiring 3 four-input ANDs with a total cost of 3*4=12.

The imbalanced decomposition of Figure 10.1 (c) can be covered optimally by 3 four-input ANDs . This shows the importance of a good decomposition for binding.

10.2

Derive a formula that yields the number of distinct decompositions of a function f, implementing the conjunction of n variable, into two-input AND gates. Tabulate the number of distinct decompositions for $n = 2, 3, \ldots, 10$.

Solution

This derivation was presented first in Reference 26. Let $f(n)$ be the number of such trees. If $n = 1$, there is only one tree consisting of a single leaf. Hence $f(1) = 1$. In $n > 1$, assume the root has i leaves under the first child, and $n - i$ under its second child, for $i = 1, 2, \ldots, \lfloor n/2 \rfloor$. (Without loss of generality, assume fewer leaves are under the first child if n is odd).

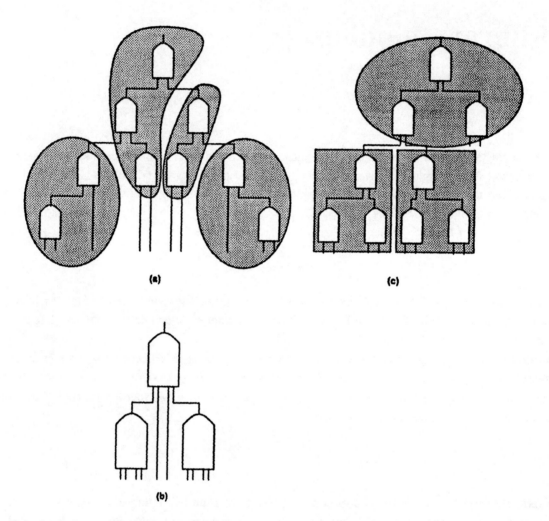

Figure 10.1: (a) Balanced decomposition and cover. (b) Best implementation. (c) Imbalanced decomposition and cover.

If $i \neq n - i$ then none of the $f(i)$ trees for the left child can be isomorphic to any of the $f(n - i)$ trees for the right child, because they have a different number of leaves. Hence, any tree formed from choosing one tree from the set for the left child and one tree from the set for the right child generates a unique tree. The number of non-isomorphic trees in this case is $f(i)f(n - i)$.

If $i = n - i$ there are fewer unique trees. Assume the $f(i)$ trees for each child are ordered. Choosing a tree for the right child with an index equal to, or greater than, the index of the tree for the left child will guarantee a unique tree. Hence there are $1/2 f(i)(f(i) + 1)$ ways of generating a unique tree in this case. The following recurrence relation computes the number of two-input AND gate trees for a network implementing the conjunction of n variables:

$$f(n) = \begin{cases} \sum_{i=1}^{\lfloor n/2 \rfloor} f(i)f(n - i) & \text{if } n \text{ is odd} \\ \sum_{i=1}^{n/2-1} f(i)f(n - i) + 1/2 f(n/2)(f(n/2) + 1) & \text{if } n \text{ is even} \end{cases}$$

The values of $f(n)$ are tabulated next.

n	$f(n)$
1	1
2	1
3	1
4	2
5	3
6	6
7	11
8	23
9	46
10	98

10.3

Consider the simple library of cells of Figure 10.8 (a). Derive all pattern trees and corresponding strings for a decomposition into NOR2 and INV base functions. Repeat the exercise by considering NOR2 , NAND2 and INV as base functions.

Solution

First we derive all pattern trees and corresponding strings using NOR2 and INV base functions. This is shown in Figure 10.2.

Second we derive all pattern trees and corresponding strings using NOR2 , NAND2 and INV base functions. Note that there are no new decompositions for OR2 and AND 2 not already shown in Figure 10.8 of the textbook or in Figure 10.2, and hence they are not repeated here. The new decompositions are shown in Figures 10.3 and 10.4.

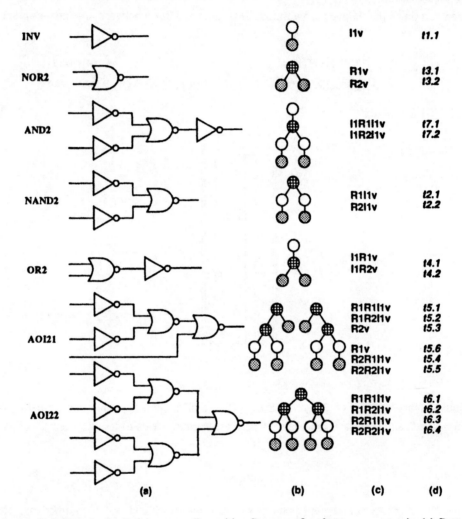

Figure 10.2: (a) Cell library. (b) Pattern trees (I = white, R = NOR2 = boxes, v = gray). (c) Pattern strings.

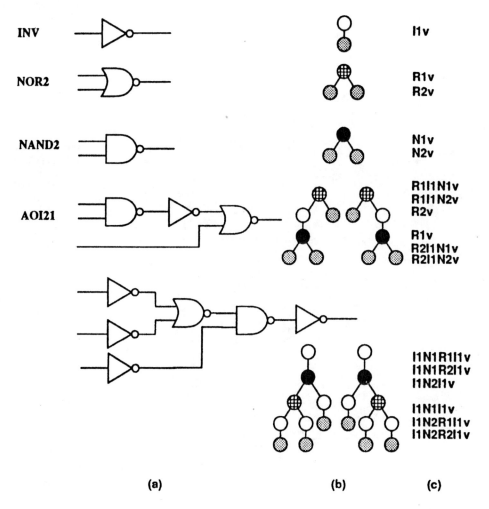

Figure 10.3: (a) Cell library. (b) Pattern trees (I = white, R = NOR2 = boxes, N = NAND2 = black, v = gray). (c) Pattern strings.

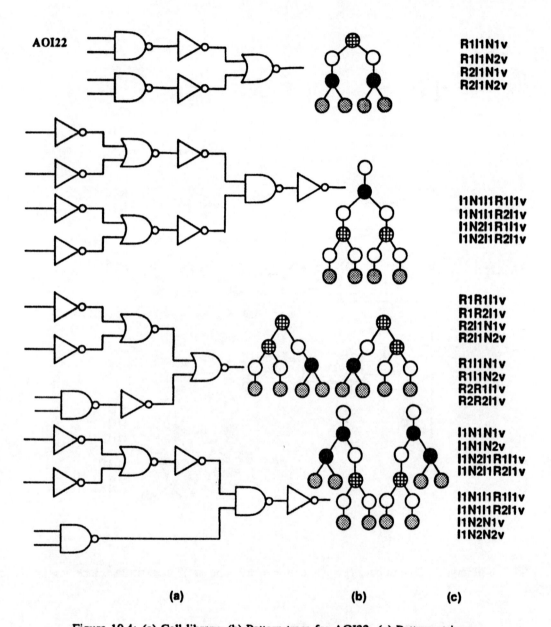

Figure 10.4: (a) Cell library. (b) Pattern trees for AOI22. (c) Pattern strings.

10.4

Consider the simple library of cells of Figure 10.8 (a) and the pattern trees according to a decomposition in NOR2 and INV (See Problem 10.3). Compute the automaton that represents the library.

Solution

The automaton that represents the library is shown in Figure 10.5.

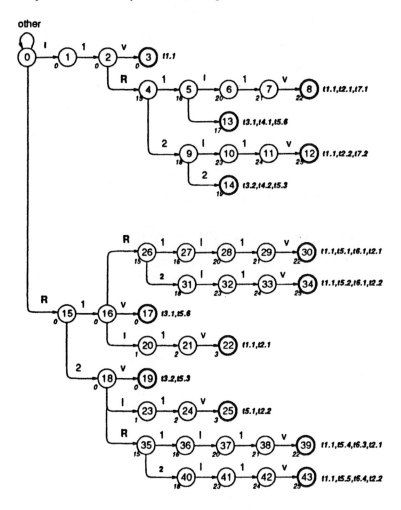

Figure 10.5: Aho-Corasick automaton for the first library of problem 3.

10.5

Consider a library including the following cells: { AND2 with cost 4; OR2 with cost 5; INV with cost 1 }. Draw the pattern trees for these cells using NAND2 and INV as base functions. Consider then function $f = ab' + c'd'b$. Determine the subject graph for f using the same base functions. Find a minimum cost cover of the subject graph using the inverter-pair heuristic.

Hint: use the following decomposition. $f = \text{NAND2}\,(p,q)$; $p = \text{NAND2}\,(a,b')$; $q = \text{NAND2}\,(c'r')$; $r = \text{NAND2}\,(d',b)$.

Solution

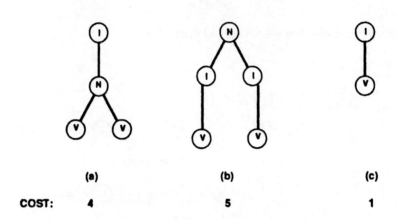

	(a)	(b)	(c)
COST:	4	5	1

Figure 10.6: Pattern trees for the three basic cells.

The pattern trees for the cells are shown in Figure 10.6. Pattern (a) is the AND2 cell, pattern (b) is the OR2 cell, and pattern (c) is the INV cell.

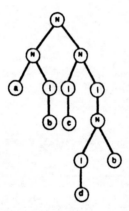

Figure 10.7: Subject graph using the NAND2 and INV base functions.

The subject graph for $f = ab' + c'd'b$ using the suggested decomposition and base functions is shown in Figure 10.7.

With the inverter-pair heuristic, we insert two inverters between every two NAND2, and add to the library an inverter pair element (called INV-INV) of cost zero. The resulting subject graph is shown in Figure 10.8, where each vertex is labeled for ease of reference.

Now we calculate the cost at each point in the cover, visiting the subject graph bottom up. We assume that inputs are available in both polarities, and so the cost of inverters on the inputs is zero. (These inverters are neglected in the computation.)

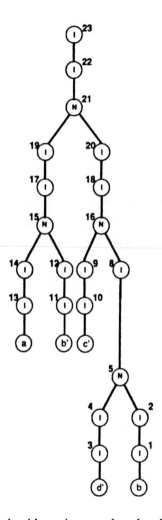

Figure 10.8: Subject graph with vertices numbered and inverter pairs inserted.

| Vertices | Component | COST | | | | Total |
		INV	AND2	OR2	INV - INV	
5	OR2 (3,1)			1		5
15	OR2 (13,11)			1		5
8	INV (5)	1		1		6
	AND2 (4,2)		1			4
17	INV (15)	1		1		6
	AND2 (14,12)		1			4
19	INV INV (15)			1	1	5
	INV (17)	1	1			5
18	AND2 (8,9)		2			8
20	INV (18)	1	2			9
21	OR2 (17,18)		3	1		17
22	INV (21)	1	3	1		18
	AND2 (19,20)	2	4		1	18
23	INV (22)	2	3	1	1	19
	INV INV (21)		3	1	1	17

The optimum solution has total cost of 17, using 3 AND2 cells and 1 OR2 cell, as expected. The solution is shown in Figure 10.9. (Note that vertex 16 does not have a feasible match, due to the fact that the base function for decomposition (NAND2) is not in in the library).

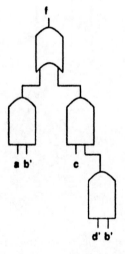

Figure 10.9: Optimum cover.

10.6

Consider a scalar function of n variables with a symmetry set set of cardinality m. How many of the cofactors of f (w.r.t. all variables in the set) differ?

Solution

For a function f with a single symmetry set of cardinality m, only $m + 1$ cofactors of f (w.r.t. all variables in the set) are different. Namely they are derived by setting $0, 1, \ldots, m$ variables to 1.

Assume now that the n variables of f are grouped into k symmetry sets of cardinality $n_1, \ldots, n_k$ (where $\sum_{i=0}^{k} n_i = n$). Then the number of distinct cofactors is $\prod_{i=0}^{k}(n_i + 1) \leq 2^n$.

10.7

Consider the library of virtual gates corresponding to static CMOS implementations of single-output functions with at most s transistors in series and p transistors in parallel. What is the size of these libraries for $s = 1, 2, \ldots, 5$, $p = 1, 2, \ldots, 5$?

Solution

We consider gates in static to CMOS technology. We consider expressions represented by Boolean Factored Forms (BFFs). Each BFF can be put in correspondence with one (or more) interconnection of transistors, that can be abstracted by two polar graphs, usually having the property of being duals of each other. We can consider then only one graph, the same consideration applying to the dual, *mutatis mutandis*. The maximum number of transistors in series s is the length of the longest path from source to sink; the maximum number of transistors in parallel p is the size of the largest cutset. Since the graph can be constructed by traversing the BFF bottom-up, these numbers can be derived from the BFF itself. Namely, the pair (s, p) is $(1, 1)$ for each leaf of a BFF. For each other vertex corresponding to a product, s is the sum of the numbers s for all sub-trees and p is the maximum of the numbers p associated with each sub-tree. The converse applies to vertices corresponding to sums. Even though many pairs of polar graphs can be associated with a BFF (i.e. all those obtained by permuting the series components), they all share the same parameters (s, p).

References 10 and 26 present a theory that leads to recursive formulae for the computation of the size of the virtual libraries that satisfy a given upper bound on s and p. It is not difficult to write a computer program, based on the aforementioned considerations, that list all the virtual gates satisfying the bound. We report the results in the following table.

(s, p)	1	2	3	4	5
1	1	2	3	4	5
2	2	7	18	42	90
3	3	18	87	396	1,677
4	4	42	396	3,503	28,435
5	5	90	1,677	28,435	425,803

10.8

Enumerate the different $\mathcal{NPN}$ classes of function of three variables, and show one representative function for each class.

Solution

There are 13 different functions, excluding tautology. Figure 10.10 shows a graph whose vertex set is in one-to-one correspondence with each class. Vertices are represented by cubes, where the minterms of a representative function are highlighted. Edges join vertex pairs that differ in one minterm.

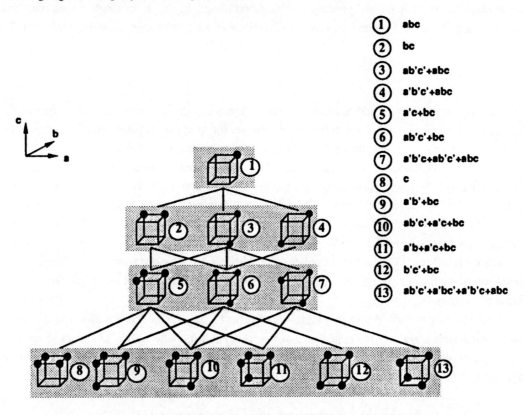

① abc
② bc
③ ab'c'+abc
④ a'b'c'+abc
⑤ a'c+bc
⑥ ab'c'+bc
⑦ a'b'c+ab'c'+abc
⑧ c
⑨ a'b'+bc
⑩ ab'c'+a'c+bc
⑪ a'b+a'c+bc
⑫ b'c'+bc
⑬ ab'c'+a'bc+a'b'c+abc

Figure 10.10: $\mathcal{NPN}$ classes of functions of three variables and representative functions.